SPORT IN DONEGAL

A HISTORY

SPORT IN DONEGAL

A HISTORY

CONOR CURRAN

First published 2010

The History Press
119 Lower Baggot Street
Dublin 2, Ireland
www.thehistorypress.ie

British Library Cataloguing in Publication Data.
A catalogue record for this book is available from the British Library.

ISBN 978 1 84588 953 1

Typesetting and origination by The History Press
Printed in Great Britain
Manufacturing managed by Jellyfish Print Solutions Ltd

CONTENTS

ACKNOWLEDGEMENTS

I would like to thank my parents and family for their constant encouragement and support, and for instilling in me a love of history as well as Gaelic football and soccer.

I am grateful to Dr James Kelly, who originally suggested that I undertake my Masters thesis on this topic, and also to my former supervisor in St Patrick's College Drumcondra, Dr Peter Martin. I am also indebted to the staff of St Patrick's College Library for their efficiency. More recently, my PhD supervisor, Professor Mike Cronin has given me much encouragement and advice, while my supervisor at De Montfort University, Professor Matthew Taylor has always been available for comment. Donal McAnallen of NUIG has been very approachable and gave me a number of ideas on the GAA in Donegal. The staffs of the National Library in Kildare Street and the National Archives in Bishop Street have been very accommodating. Those working in the UCD Folklore Commission, Delargy Centre, also deserve thanks for their help, and I would also like to express my gratitude to my good friends Nicola Doogan and Jean Hughes for their support and advice.

At home, Edward Molloy has provided me with a wealth of literature on Gaelic games in the county, while Mary McHugh supplied me with a number of books which were very useful. John McConnell was always willing to pass on information and brought a number of photographs for this book to my attention. Don Byrne provided me with a great insight into the Evans family history, and John Gildea and Molly Gallagher took time to discuss the early days of Gaelic football and soccer in Ardara with me. Jim Deeny of Rathmullan, a descendant of a prominent figure in the history of soccer in Donegal, has also been very helpful. Sean Beattie of the Donegal Historical Society was very encouraging and I am grateful to him for allowing me to publish material in the 2008 Annual. The Revd John Deane and Canon Austin Laverty gave me access to church records at quite short notice, it must be added. The staff of the Central Library in Letterkenny have been very helpful, and those working in the Raphoe Diocesan Archives took time out to allow me to view the papers of Cardinal O'Donnell. Niamh Brennan of the Donegal County Archives in Lifford was very accommodating, and Helen Meehan provided me with much information on Seumas MacManus. Moira Mallon proved to be very informative on the Killybegs Emeralds.

Journalists Frank Craig and Damian Dowds were always available for advice. Ballyshannon historian Anthony Begley discussed his locality at length with me, and John Ward and Carol Briscoe were both quick to respond to requests for information about the *Donegal Vindicator* newspaper. I am also grateful to Eamonn Monaghan for his advice on the first Donegal GAA county board. Chris Cameron of the Celtic Visitors' Centre in Glasgow pointed me in the direction of sources of which I was unaware, while Tom Plunkett and Eddie O'Donnell have also brought a number of local history issues to my attention. Janet O'Donnell, Malachi McCloskey, and Joe and Dympna Duff have helped ease my difficult quest to obtain photographs.

I am also very grateful to Finbar Jordan and Ronan Colgan of The History Press Ireland for giving me the opportunity to write this book. Finally, I would like to thank my fiancée Jessica for her patience and kindness throughout my study of sports history over the past few years, for her computer expertise, and for sharing with me many hours of the History Channel and ESPN Classic!

ABBREVIATIONS

AGM: Annual General Meeting
AOH: Ancient Order of Hibernians
CC: Catholic Curate
CE: Civil Engineer
DC: District Clerk
DJ: *Derry Journal*
DI: District Inspector
DI: *Donegal Independent*
DL: Deputy Lieutenant
DV: *Donegal Vindicator*
GAA: Gaelic Athletic Association
FA: Football Association
FC: Football Club
HMS: His Majesty's Ship
IFA: Irish Football Association
IRO: Inland Revenue Officer
JP: Justice of Peace
NS: National School
TD: Teachta Dála

INTRODUCTION

In March 1914, the Ireland soccer team won the Home championship after a draw with Scotland, having defeated England and Wales over a three-week period.[1] Writing in *Association football and society in pre-partition Ireland*, Neal Garnham claims that in Ireland, 'the progress of the game had been aided by a number of factors, while others had served to impede it. The result of this was the uneven growth and spread of the game, both chronologically and geographically.'[2] This could be said of the development of soccer, and indeed of Gaelic games, in Donegal. Because of the apparent discrepancies between the popularity of, and the lack of interest in, the various sports played throughout Donegal, this book aims to analyse not only the causes of this, but also the reasons why certain sports held sway in some areas of the county as opposed to others. Also, from a sociological perspective, I feel it is essential to examine some of the ways in which sport acted as a developmental agent for various communities throughout the county in the period 1881-1914. It is important to examine the development of organised sport in Donegal in comparison with other areas, and, although the country was part of Britain up until 1921, it must be noted that a number of factors which helped the development of sport across the water played little or no part in the emergence of organised sporting competitions in Ireland.

Sports historian Mike Cronin, while noting that Ireland lagged far behind mainland Britain in terms of industrial development at the end of the nineteenth century, has stated that agriculture was the 'dominant means of production', with 'the long-term effects of the Great Famine' hampering the development of the economy in the former nation with the exception of parts of Ulster. He also claims that 'the absence of modernising forces across most of Ireland meant that many of the social and economic changes, which would empower the sporting revolution in Britain, were absent'.[3] This meant that 'key innovations' such as the Ten Hours Act, which paved the way for an increase in spare time for workers, 'did not have a great impact' in Ireland, where the dominance of the Catholic Church (outside Ulster) also meant that Sunday, rather than Saturday, was seen as the day for recreation.[4]

Cronin also believes that the class structure which played a significant part in the development of sport in Britain, with the dissemination of sport by past students, could not be replicated in Ireland, as the education structure was not the same, and that, 'the landed, moneyed and industrial elite had no interest in encouraging the leisure of the masses' in Ireland as had taken place with the development of working-class sports' clubs in Britain.[5] However, although the development of the GAA was helped by its nationalist identity, it benefited from its modelling of the British-type codification of sport and the encouraging of 'muscular Christianity and manliness in similar fashion to British sports'.[6] These views will be looked at in terms of the development of both the GAA and soccer in Donegal.

It could be argued that the clubs involved in the first Donegal Football Association Challenge Cup in 1894, who were almost all from north and north-east Donegal (the exception being Derrybeg Celtic in the north-west) came from areas which are the bedrock of soccer in the county today.

In the 2009 season there were no teams from the west coast of Donegal in the Ulster Senior League, the highest level of competitive soccer in Donegal. Of the eleven competing clubs, ten were from the north or north-east of the county, with Derry City also fielding a team.

Therefore, I will attempt to trace the origins of a number of early soccer clubs in Donegal. The political climate at the beginning of the twentieth century must be carefully examined, as it is clear that the foundation of the Donegal GAA county board in 1905 came at the time that Tom Garvin has described as 'a new cultural nationalism'.[7] One must carefully assess the reasons for the growth and decline of a number of the clubs involved in this first attempt to establish a GAA county board in the county, along with their geographical locations, as it is clear that Gaelic football is now the most popular sport in the south and south-west of the county, but this was not always the case. Of the sixteen clubs that have won the Dr Maguire Cup (the Donegal Gaelic football senior championship), eleven have been from the south or south-west and only four from the east. No club from Inishowen has ever won it, and Gweedore, with their fourteen victories, are the only club from the north-west of the county to claim the trophy.

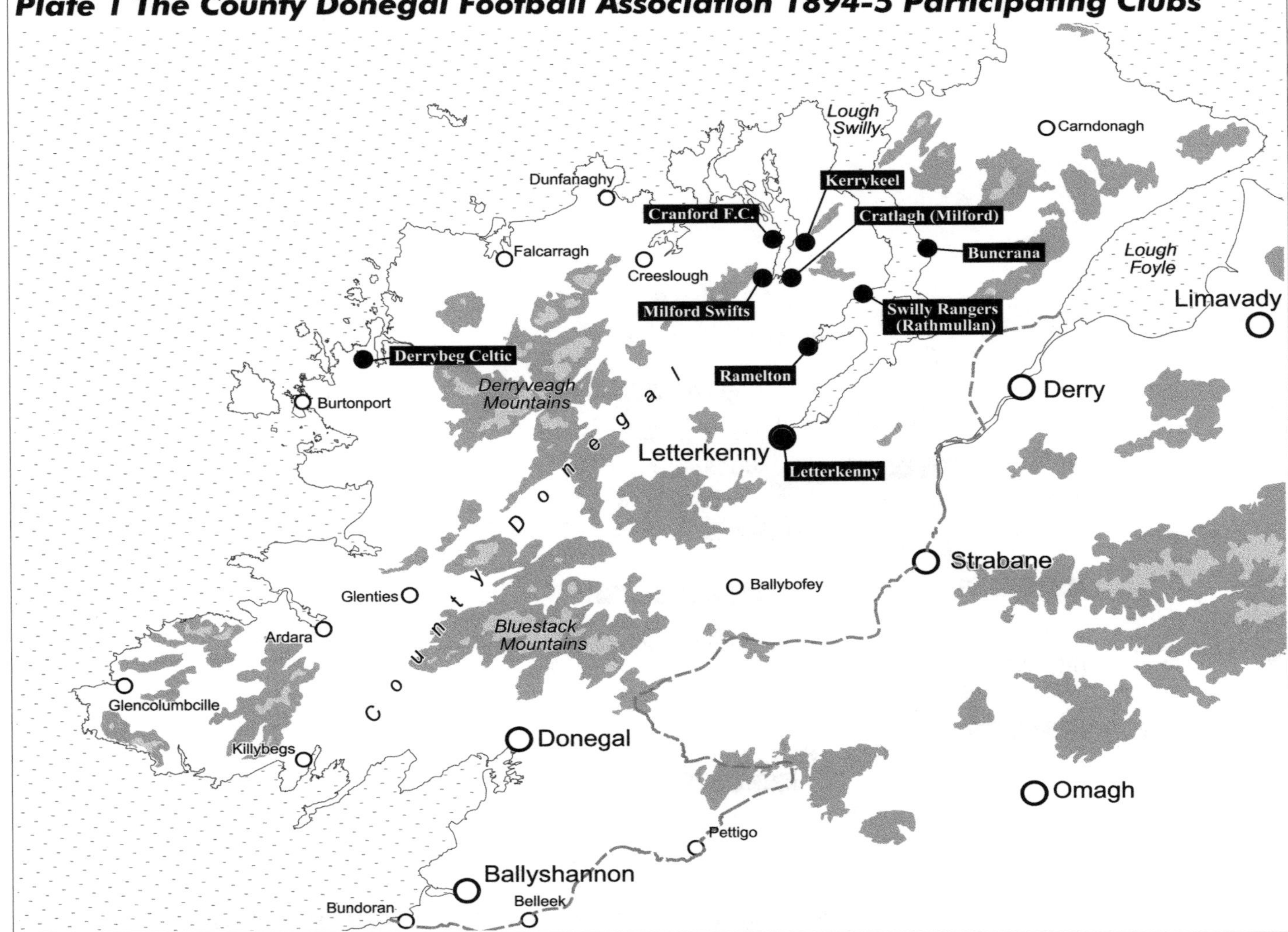

Plate 1 The County Donegal Football Association 1894-5 Participating Clubs
Lough Swilly
Carndonagh
Dunfanaghy
Kerrykeel
Cranford F.C.
Cratlagh (Milford)
Buncrana
Falcarragh
Creeslough
Lough Foyle
Milford Swifts
Swilly Rangers (Rathmullan)
Limavady
Derrybeg Celtic
Ramelton
Derryveagh Mountains
Burtonport
Derry
County Donegal
Letterkenny
Letterkenny
Strabane
Glenties
Ballybofey
Ardara
Bluestack Mountains
Glencolumbcille
Donegal
Killybegs
Omagh
Pettigo
Ballyshannon
Bundoran
Belleek

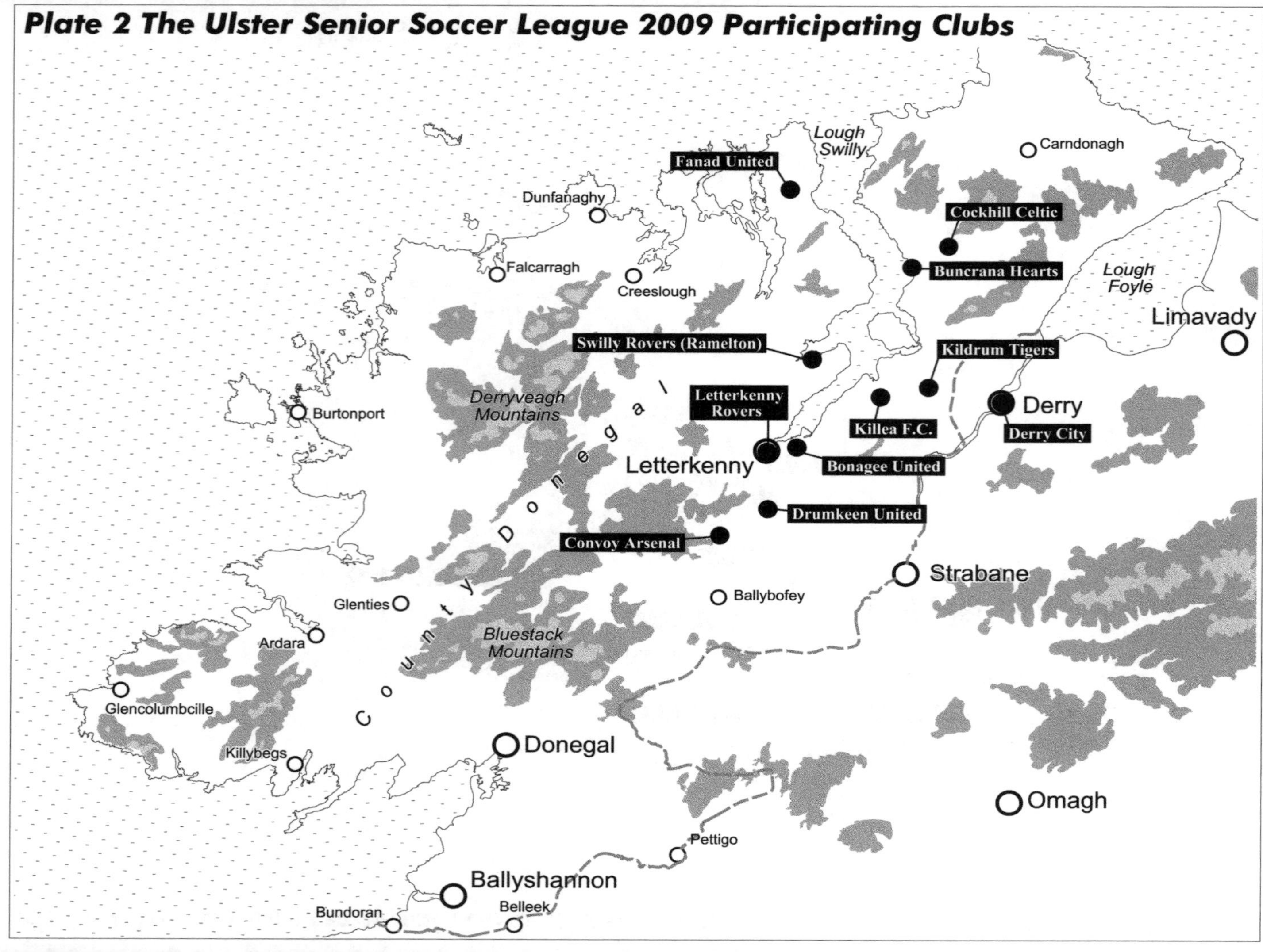

Plate 2 The Ulster Senior Soccer League 2009 Participating Clubs

By early 1906, it was claimed that the eastern division of the newly founded Donegal GAA county board was lagging behind the western division in its Gaelic games activities, as illustrated in the Derry Journal.[8] By mid-1907, both divisions were in serious decline, and the county board was not re-established until 1919. In contrast to the Ulster Senior soccer league, in 2009, seven of the nine clubs in Division 1 of the Donegal Gaelic football league were located near the west coast, with the exception of Glenswilly and St Eunan's from Letterkenny in the north-east of the county.

This illustrates the strength of the western and south/south-western GAA clubs, and the popularity of Gaelic football in these areas. However, the last number of years have seen a shift in the popularity of Gaelic football in the north of the county, with the emergence of clubs such as Termon, Glenswilly and St Michael's of Dunfanaghy, and in the selection of players from non-traditional GAA areas in the county for the Donegal senior Gaelic football team.

Cross-country hurling was particularly prominent in various areas throughout the county in the late 1800s and at the start of the twentieth century, as recorded in the Folklore Commission archives by Seán Ó hEochaidh and in the work of Ardara club historian Pádraig S. Mac a' Ghoill, and its decline must be addressed, along with the reasons for the hurling success and tradition enjoyed by the Burt club in Inishowen. In addition to this, I will examine a number of reasons for the lack of prominence of the Donegal hurling team on a national stage. The codification or systematic organisation of rules within Gaelic games must also be looked at, as it is clear that the origins of both hurling and Gaelic football have been subverted by a number of GAA writers in their works. This was a recurring theme at the beginning of the twentieth century in the GAA notes of the Donegal press, as it was not uncommon for those involved in the organisation of the GAA to attack what they perceived to be elements of West British culture. According to W.F. Mandle, 'the GAA from the start took great pains to emphasise the distinctiveness and long history of Irish sport'.[9] This was necessary, those within the organisation felt, 'to counter the moral and historical overtones that went with the games revolution, overtones that emphasised the character-building worth of team games and their essential usefulness to, even precondition of, England's imperial mission, something to which Irishmen would be particularly sensitive'.[10]

Those involved in soccer came under attack in Donegal after the donation of the Evans Cup to the Ardara Emeralds Football Club for local competition in January 1905, and the role played by various nationalist organisations in this conflict must not be overlooked. This anti-soccer view was not uncommon amongst

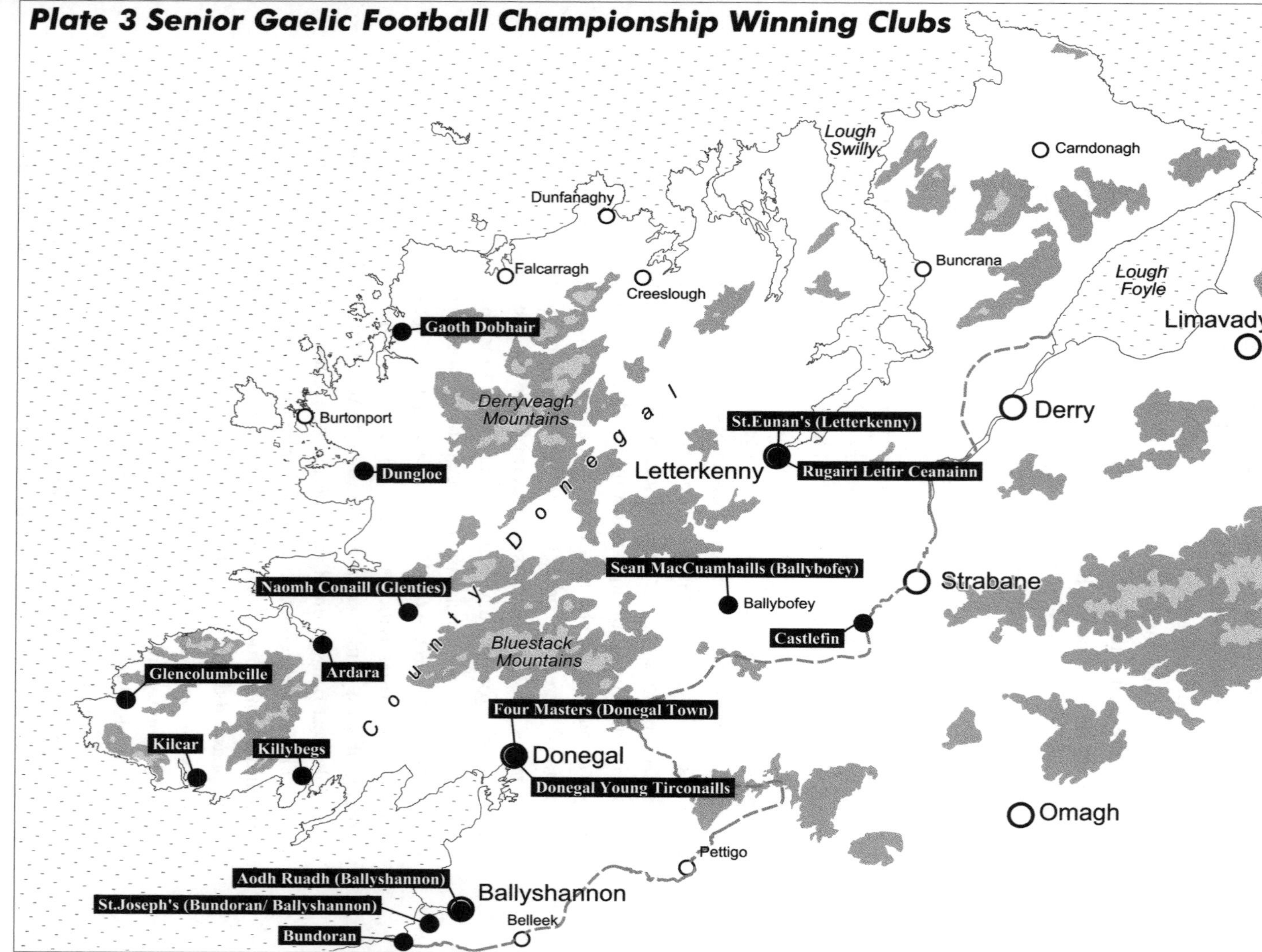

Plate 3 Senior Gaelic Football Championship Winning Clubs

those involved in patriotic associations in other counties such as Fermanagh[11] and so the role of nationalist activist and writer Seumas MacManus in Donegal must be taken into consideration. Also of interest are the efforts of Cardinal Patrick O'Donnell, who, according to the *Derry Journal* after his death in 1927, 'never lost an opportunity of showing his sympathy with the ideals of the Gaelic Athletic Association [while Bishop of Raphoe]'.[12] The influence of the clergy in sports organisations, and their efforts to promote the Temperance movement, meant that a number of sporting clubs in Donegal were favourable to the teetotal principle. Neal Garnham states that soccer acted as 'a great temperate reformer' and at the turn of the century local matches kept men 'away from the public-house and its baneful influences'.[13]

In 1911, the Catholic population in the Laggan area was between 50 and 65 per cent of the total number of people living there and the region was largely associated with farming and the hiring fair in Letterkenny, which was held every May and November.[14] The religious affiliation of the people of Donegal can go some way towards explaining the popularity of cricket in the east of the county, as clubs competing in the County Donegal Cricket League in 1895 were all from areas lying in or near the Laggan Valley (although this is not to say that there were no cricket clubs in the west of the county in this decade).

In the north of the county, Lough Swilly was an important port which remained under British control until 1938 and, according to Donal Campbell, 'some people hold the view that the British Army Forts which surrounded the Swilly were a primary force in the popularisation of soccer in the area'.[15]

Financial accounts of soccer and GAA organisations in the county and records of attendances at events and membership figures will also be examined, as clubs' survival depended largely on having successful accounts. It must be noted that the attendances at these sporting events are, of course, estimates and at times were grossly exaggerated in the local press. Caution must be exercised, therefore, as 'gates' were seldom accounted for properly.

It is also important to examine the lives of those who were involved in the founding of clubs, as these people were often those with local businesses or positions of influence and authority in local societies. Their money and spare time were significant factors in the development of organisational committees, along with a passion for their preferred sport and their town or village. Indeed, many of these patrons saw it as their duty in the development of local society, with the donating of cups and medals and the granting of access to their fields being fundamental to the growth of competitive sport, long before clubs were able to own their own pitches.

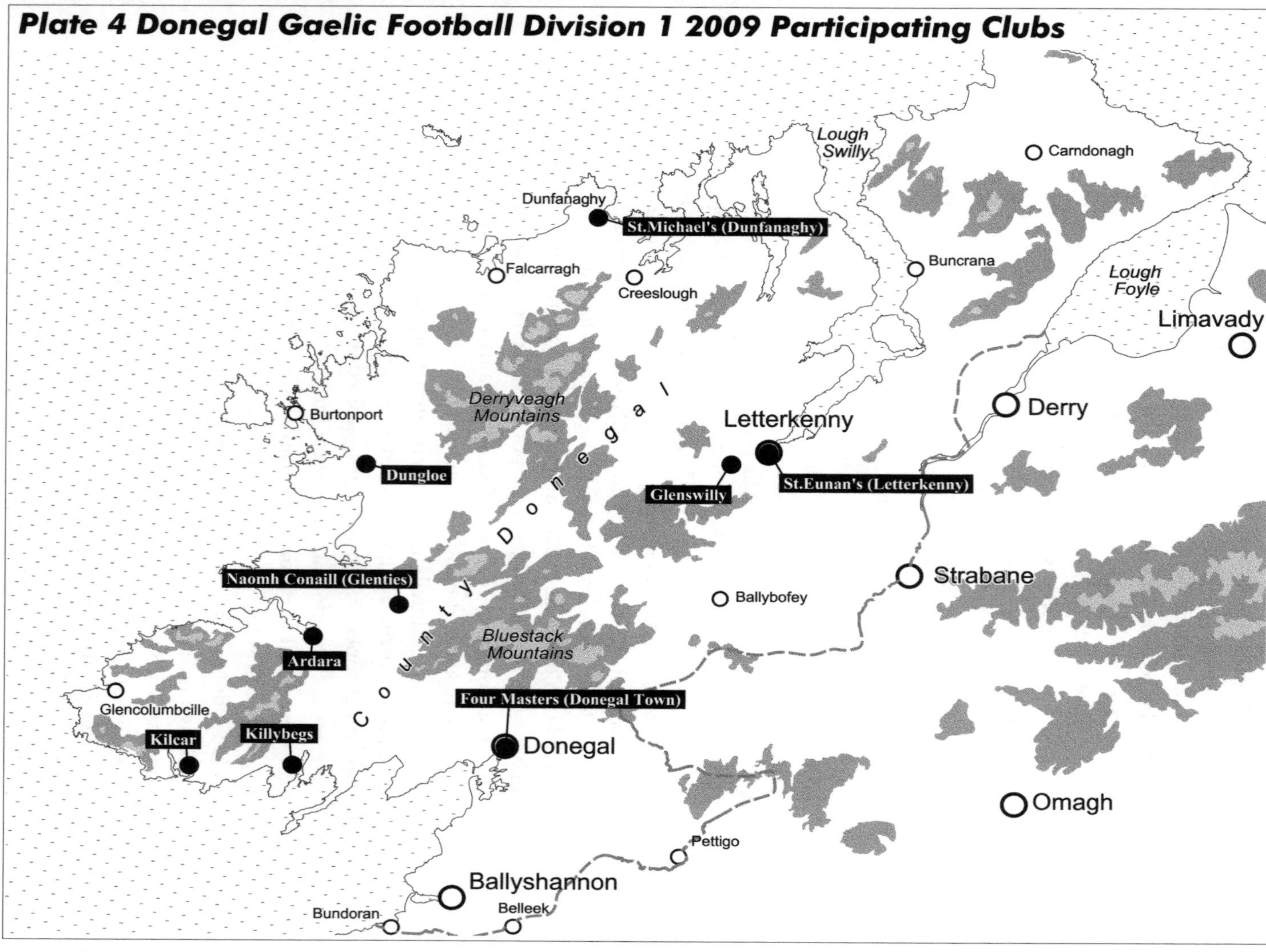

Plate 4 Donegal Gaelic Football Division 1 2009 Participating Clubs

Horse racing also attracted much interest in the 1890s and regattas were well attended along the Donegal coastline towards the end of the nineteenth century. Rugby, cricket, hockey and handball also featured from time to time in the local newspapers, but this work will focus primarily on Gaelic games and soccer. To date, the development of these codes and indeed sport in Donegal has attracted little academic attention, and as Paul Rouse has noted, 'Irish historians have contrived gross generalisations to explain the country's sporting past.'[16] He feels that they have a general tendency to 'focus on the Gaelic Athletic Association to the exclusion of every other sporting body. Further, even that organisation is assessed only through the prism of politics and invariably without research worthy of the name.'[17] The growth of soccer in Ireland has been traced by Neal Garnham, but focuses mainly on events in Belfast and Dublin and the development of the Irish Football Association. John Sugden and Alan Bairner have investigated the relationship between sport and politics in Northern Ireland and the development of sport in the Republic but without much analysis on Donegal. In 2004 Ardara GAA club published *Idir Peil agus Pobal*,[18] which is perhaps the most detailed study of any sporting club in Donegal, despite productions of note by two other GAA clubs which cover the period in this publication: Kilcar, who in 1984 published *CLG Cill Chartha*,[19] which traces the origins of the south-west club prior to its foundation in 1924 and up until the GAA's centenary year, and *Against the Grain*[20] (2000), which looks at the history of Burt and its GAA club. The Ardara book was originally researched by the late Pádraig S. Mac a' Ghoill and chronicles the club's history from the beginning of the twentieth century until 2004. Mac a' Ghoill also contributed a number of articles on Gaelic games to the *Donegal Historical Annual*. Fr Seán Ó Gallchóir is widely recognised as the county's leading authority on the Donegal senior Gaelic football championship, having published several books on the subject. A short summary of the early days of the GAA in Donegal was printed in 1997 by Mountcharles man Eamonn Monaghan, but there have been no academic publications to date.[21]

A number of soccer clubs, such as Donegal Town FC and Swilly Rovers, have produced books chronicling their recent histories, but as yet there has been no book published on the early history of organised soccer in Donegal. In 1996, St Catherine's of Killybegs published their club history to mark 100 years of soccer in the town, but there has been no written account of the County Donegal Football Association to date.

The nationalist newspaper the *Derry Journal* has provided a valuable insight into the rivalry between association football and Gaelic games at the beginning

Plate 5 Clubs Participating in the County Donegal Cricket League 1895

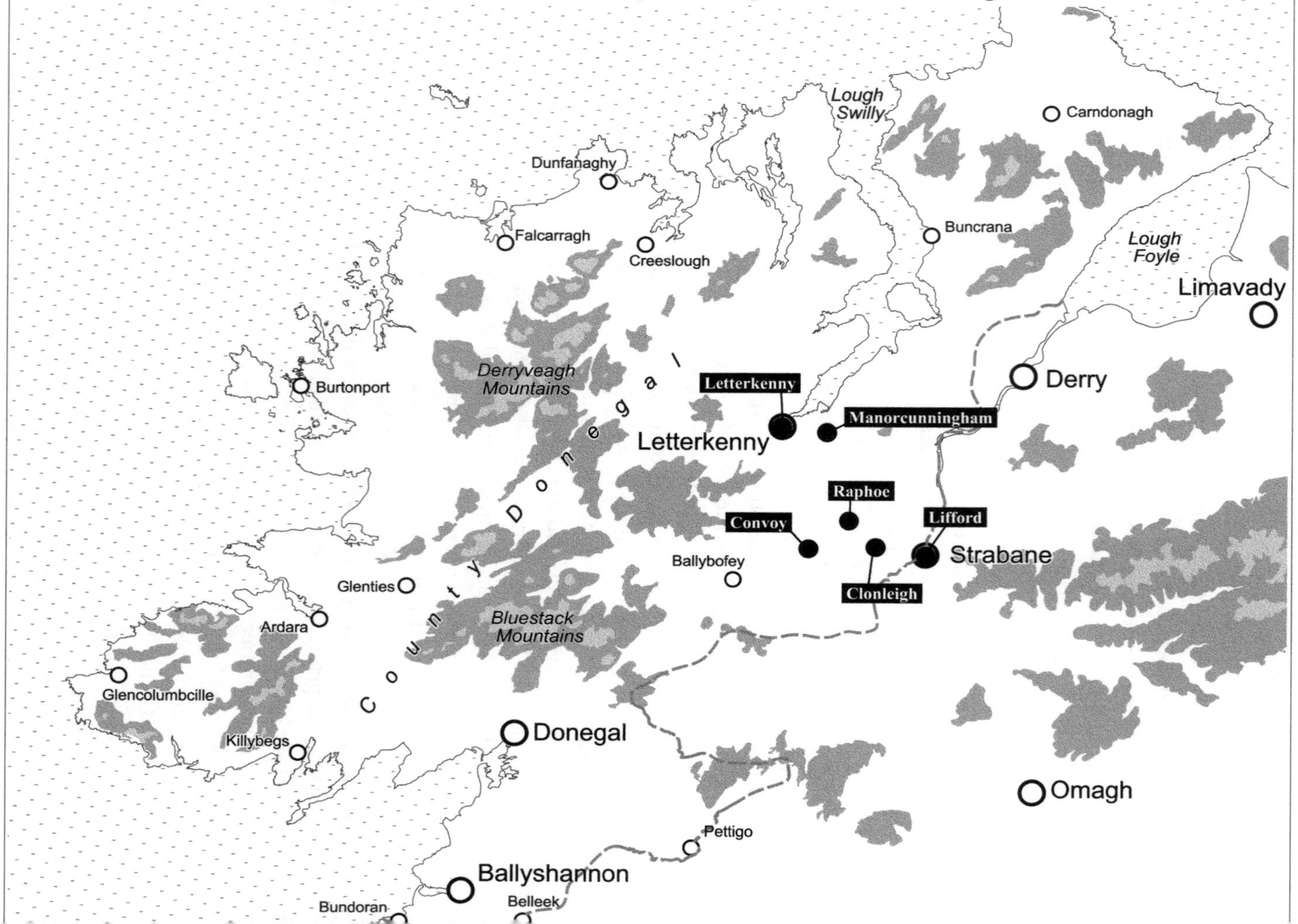

Lough Swilly
Carndonagh
Dunfanaghy
Buncrana
Falcarragh
Creeslough
Lough Foyle
Limavady
Derryveagh Mountains
Burtonport
Letterkenny
Manorcunningham
Letterkenny
Derry
County Donegal
Raphoe
Convoy
Lifford
Strabane
Ballybofey
Clonleigh
Glenties
Ardara
Bluestack Mountains
Glencolumbcille
Killybegs
Donegal
Omagh
Pettigo
Ballyshannon
Belleek
Bundoran

of the twentieth century, although at times results and reports of activities were discontinued. Both the *Donegal Independent* and *Donegal Vindicator* sports reports focused mainly on activities in the south of the county and covered the growth of competitions in soccer in Ballyshannon, as well as Gaelic games in this area. Nationally, local sports news from this era can be found sporadically in Dublin newspaper *The Sport* and the *Freeman's Journal*, although the frequency of this depended on the enthusiasm of club secretaries. Local newspaper reports are often difficult to judge, often depending on the writers' political and sporting interests. This is, at times, frustrating for researchers, as reports on competitions such as the Donegal FA Challenge Cup in 1898 and the Britton Cup in 1914 were discontinued when the enthusiasm of both reporters and newspaper editors respectively waned. It is also worth noting that, while evidence of clubs matches and competitions is sufficient to draw a general chronology and analysis of soccer and Gaelic games in the years covered in this book, not every match was recorded in the press and the existence of teams varied from occasional challenge matches to full seasons of competition.

The records of the Royal Irish Constabulary illustrate their monitoring of organisations such as the GAA and the movements of IRB suspect Seumas MacManus, but unfortunately go into little detail regarding activities of early Donegal GAA clubs. A GAA archive has recently been established in Lifford but it only covers material from 1927 onwards.

An interesting history of the sport of handball in Donegal has been published by Pat Holland, and despite the fact that the sport has never reached the levels of popularity enjoyed by soccer or Gaelic football in the county, there has been sporadic participation around Donegal, most notably in Gaeltacht areas along the coast, such as Falcarragh and Glencolumbkille.

Chapter one will look at early forms of hurling in Donegal and the first GAA clubs in the county. It also addresses the state of Donegal society in the 1880s and the reasons why Gaelic games were slow to develop there. Chapter two traces the beginning of association football in Donegal and looks at the founding of a number of clubs. In chapter three the events which led to the foundation of the first Donegal GAA county board will be addressed and the successes and failures of this will be analysed. Chapter four looks at the decline of the Donegal GAA county board and the growth of competitive soccer in south Donegal.

It is hoped that this work will help shed some light on the state of Gaelic games and soccer in the county during the late Victorian and early Edwardian years and, in painting a picture of society in these times, will also contribute to the historiography of Donegal for the period 1881–1914.

1

THE GEOGRAPHY OF DONEGAL, DONEGAL SOCIETY AND THE EARLY DAYS OF GAELIC GAMES IN THE COUNTY

'*It should be remembered that there are two Donegals – an outer and an inner.*'[1]

Revd G.A. Lecky

DONEGAL IN THE LATE NINETEENTH CENTURY

In order to assess the role played by Gaelic games and soccer in Donegal society from 1881 to 1914, one must look carefully at the geography of the county and at the social divisions which were evident at the time. In 1881, the population of Donegal was 206,035. Of these people, 76 per cent were Roman Catholic, 12 per cent belonged to the Church of Ireland, 10 per cent belonged to the Presbyterian Church, and 1 per cent were Methodists.[2] Donegal belonged to what was known as 'the other Ulster', and according to Jim MacLaughlin, this was, 'the overwhelmingly Catholic and underdeveloped west of the province, a region that was of peripheral interest to Ulster unionists but of considerable strategic and symbolic significance to Irish nationalists ever anxious to acquire "lebensraum" or "living space", for an Irish Catholic nation'.[3] The economic and religious divisions in the county were rather contrastingly illustrated by the Revd G.A. Lecky, writing in his book *In the Days of the Laggan presbytery*, which was published in 1908:

> It should be remembered that there are two Donegals – an outer and an inner. The former, which is almost wholly Roman Catholic, and from which the county to a large extent takes its character and complexion in the eye of the

public, consists of extensive mountainous districts that lie along the western seaboard, and at some points run far inland. The latter consists of the more flat and fertile country that lies between the mountains and the River Foyle – the eastern boundary of the county. It is largely Protestant and from a very early period in history has been known as the Laggan, i.e. the low and level country.[4]

EAST DONEGAL

It was in this area that 'the land was better, the holdings larger and the tenants enjoyed the fixity of tenure which had become known as "the Ulster custom"'.[5] Towns such as Lifford, Letterkenny, Raphoe, Convoy, Ballybofey and Stranorlar all lie in this area, which has the most arable land in the county. Association football was gaining popularity in this area in the 1890s, but cricket had been enjoyed there for a number of years prior to this. By 1891, the East Donegal Cricket Union was up and running, and the final tie took place on Saturday 20 August between Ballybofey and Lifford in Convoy 'to decide which would have the honour of lifting the pot for the first time'.[6] Convoy, St Johnston, Raphoe, Manorcunningham, Lifford and Ballybofey had all entered the competition that summer[7] and Lifford, with a strong military influence in their team, won by seven wickets; they paraded the trophy on the train that evening and were well received on their arrival home.[8] While it is difficult to establish when exactly this organisation was founded, there is evidence that cricket clubs had been established in east Donegal by 1865.[9]

WEST DONEGAL

The difficulties faced by those interested in hosting sport in west Donegal in the nineteenth century were highlighted in a report of the Rosses Regatta, which was held at Maghery on the west coast of Donegal in July 1876, 'Notwithstanding the remoteness of the locality, the sparseness of the population, the comparative absence of wealthy, influential gentlemen, and the difficulties in getting up popular amusements consequent on these drawbacks, the sports of Thursday must be a chronicled success.'[10]

In the Catholic-dominated west of the county, most people did not enjoy the prosperous type of lifestyle enjoyed by many farmers in the Laggan. Home industries such as knitting, tweed making and embroidery were commonplace, and 'these cottage industries involved considerable numbers of people but for many of the workers they provided bare economic survival rather than the build-up of modest prosperity'.[11] The physical barrier of the Derryveagh and Blue Stack mountains further widened the economic and social divides between east and west Donegal. Pat Bolger also believes that 'the most striking feature of west Donegal was the close interaction with Scotland mediated through the large-scale annual migration in search of work'.[12] Agricultural labouring employment was plentiful in the Lothian area of Scotland, where it was not uncommon for Donegal families to seek work.[13] Bolger claims that:

> ...the official statistics [based on 'male landless labourers' migrating to Scotland] are notoriously inaccurate, but the trend was towards an increased migration during the 1890s, peaking at a notional 2,500 in 1899. The Poor Law Union of Dunfanaghy had a migration rate of 45.6 per 1,000, with the Glenties Union at 35.8.[14]

This level of migration was significant in the slow development of Gaelic games and soccer in the county as, according to Neil Tranter, generally, 'the more industrial and commercial the economy the greater the extent of organised sport and the earlier its inception',[15] and Donegal was certainly slow to develop as an industrialised area in comparison to mainland Britain.

INDUSTRY AND EDUCATION IN DONEGAL

Jim MacLaughlin has claimed that in the 1880s the county 'was untouched by the hand of modern industry' and 'setting foot in Donegal was like entering a time warp. Here there was "no time" and "no call to know the clock".'[16] According to Paul Rouse, 'in the Irish countryside ... the fall in population and the relative failure to industrialise did not prove inimical to sporting development'.[17] He also believes that, 'Belfast most closely resembled the northern industrial cities of England with its professional soccer leagues and working-class sporting culture', while rugby, cricket, tennis and golf were popular among the wealthier classes in Dublin.[18] Rouse also feels, however, that improved literacy rates and the development of the railway network were important factors in the dissemination of sporting news in rural Ireland prior to the Great War.[19] Donegal in the 1880s was primarily an agricultural society and lacked the educational institutes so often associated with the diffusion of sport in the sporting revolution, and according to Helen Meehan, 'only a very small number of Donegal people received post primary education before the 20th century'.[20] Many children in west Donegal were forced to take up seasonal migration duties, working on farms in the Laggan, and it was noted that school attendances in the Rosses were of an unsatisfactory nature in the early 1890s.[21]

Second-level education was practically non-existent in the county, with only a small number of establishments of this type in the Diocese of Raphoe in 1891, these being the Literary Institute in Letterkenny, the Royal School in Raphoe and the Prior School in Lifford. In tracing the influence of Cardinal O'Donnell on Donegal society, Dr Pádraig Ó Baoighill has established that the Letterkenny institute 'was run by three priests and twenty-two young men were being prepared for the pursuit of philosophy in major seminaries such as Maynooth, Carlow and Kilkenny'.[22] The Royal School in Raphoe had been set up along with four others in the province in 1608, and the Prior Endowed School in Lifford, founded in the 1880s, amalgamated with this in the 1970s. There is little evidence that any of these placed a strong emphasis on sport in the late nineteenth century. Donegal, of course, had no third-level establishments. Trinity College had been the only university in Ireland until the 1840s and Trinity students were mainly of the Church of Ireland denomination.

Neil Tranter has stated that the theory behind the 'downwards social diffusionist model' was that 'organised forms of sport originated in the most prestigious of the elite public schools' in Britain.[23] These games eventually spread from the middle classes to the working classes, 'either through the influence of emulation or the proselytizing endeavours of former public school-boys and university alumni'.[24] While the educational and class system in Ireland differed vastly from that in Britain, the general lack of opportunity for most Donegal people to participate in second and third-level education in the nineteenth century, therefore, further delayed the spread of organised, codified sport into Donegal society.

More recently, Matthew Taylor has claimed that 'more research is needed before we can be confident of grasping the intricacies of football's geographical and social diffusion' towards the end of the nineteenth century.[25] He feels that the 'complex and often contradictory patterns' that have been noted in areas of Britain were not uncommon in the spread of association football in Ireland.[26] It is highly likely that the founder of the Donegal FA in 1894, Daniel Deeney from Rathmullan, may have had some experience of soccer while studying to become a teacher in St Patrick's College, Drumcondra. A schoolboys' league was also set up in the Rathmullan area for national school children at the end of 1896, but this appears to have been a brief affair.[27]

LINKS WITH SCOTLAND

Glasgow was an important area for Donegal migrants for finding employment and it was at the parish hall of the Catholic area, St Mary's, that Glasgow Celtic Football Club was founded on 6 November 1887 at a meeting which was to have 'enormous repercussions for the Catholic community of Glasgow'.[28] According to Chris Cameron of the Celtic Visitors' Centre, the majority of the initial committee members were said to 'be either Irish, or of Irish parentage, but the difficult part is tracing back exactly where in Ireland they, or their parents, came from.'[29] This is because many club records from the nineteenth century were destroyed in a fire in 1928. However, a number of important points regarding the Glasgow club's foundation were recorded in the book *The Story of the Celtic*, written by their manager Willie Maley in 1939. Maley had been at the club since its beginning and recorded that:

> ... a famous family in those days was the Macreadies, 'Old Dominic' of that ilk having a very popular bar in Saltmarket, where all of the youth of Donegal came for a job when they landed off the 'palatial' boats, which in those days did alike for human beings and cattle. Three of the Macreadies stuck to the new venture, and John Macreadie acted on [the] committee for three years.[30]

In 1892, a sod containing Donegal shamrocks was laid in the centre of the club's new ground, Celtic Park, by Irish National Land League founder Michael Davitt,[31] a man whose family were believed to be descendants from the McDevitt family in Inishowen, a number of whom took part in the Flight of the Earls.[32] Although this sod was later stolen, it is clear that there were strong Donegal connections with Celtic FC from the beginning.[33] Many Irish labourers were involved in drainage works in Glasgow, and Maley believed they were ambitious to get involved in the running of a team in the city.[34] The club was patronised by Archbishop Eyre, who stated that it was formed to raise funds for feeding the poor children of Glasgow's East End.[35]

Cameron also believes that, 'alongside Brother Walfrid, John Glass is undoubtedly the most important individual in the formation of the club … although he was born in Glasgow his parents were said to be of Donegal stock'.[36] By September 1895, there were two teams from west Donegal competing in the newly formed County Donegal Football Association Challenge Cup: Derrybeg Celtic from Gweedore and Kincasslagh Shamrocks from the Rosses. It is evident that those living in and migrating from these areas took inspiration from the Scottish team in their organising and playing of association football. The Celtic Football Club served as a badge of identity for these Donegal people arriving in Scotland and to this day, the club has a large support base in Donegal.[37]

Seasonal workers and returning emigrants have been identified as being fundamental to the spread of association football in the Rosses area in the latter half of the 1890s.[38] Although unrecorded in the three local papers at the time, another significant west Donegal club, Keadue Rovers, later made famous by former Irish international goalkeeper Packie Bonner, was formed in April 1896 by two brothers, Maurice and Con Campbell, who had played for St John's of Perth.[39] The Keadue team participated in matches against other local sides such as Cruit, Kincasslagh, Braide, Annagry, Mullaghduff, Maghery, Marameelan, Arranmore and Gweedore around this time.[40]

The Rosses has been described as, 'the name given to the combined civil parishes of Templecrone and Lettermacaward, in North-west Donegal', with Dungloe the only town in this area.[41] North of this area lie the parishes of Gweedore and Cloughaneely, which make up the north-west of the county. Agriculturally, this is a poor, rocky area, with a number of islands such as Arranmore (The Rosses) and Tory relying primarily on the fishing industry. The setting up of the Congested District Board relaunched the fishing industry in Donegal in early 1895 and this helped alleviate the famine which was prevalent in the county at the time.[42]

SOUTH-WEST, SOUTH AND NORTH DONEGAL

The south-west area was badly affected by the famine, with much of the population from areas such as Glencolumbkille, Kilcar, Ardara and Glenties suffering from the failure of the potato crop. From the Eany River, in the parish of Inver, to the River Drowes in Bundoran, this area of south Donegal contains the towns of Donegal, Ballyshannon and Bundoran, and the villages of Mountcharles, Laghey and Ballintra. In 1891, Ballyshannon, with a population of 2,471, was the largest town in County Donegal and throughout the 1890s the infantry were housed at the Rock Barracks there.[43] Therefore, the involvement of the town's military in sporting affairs must not be ignored. Similarly, the town's Church of Ireland contingent was largely responsible for the organisation of hunting, cricket and tennis clubs in the area in the latter part of the nineteenth century.

The Inishowen Peninsula, in the north of the county, lies between the Swilly River and the Foyle, with Malin Head the most northerly point in Donegal. Carndonagh and Buncrana are the main towns in this area, which includes Burt, and it is in close proximity to Derry and so some of the early sporting interests of these areas will also be examined.

THE SLOW DEVELOPMENT OF THE GAA IN DONEGAL

There is no record of any Gaelic football, soccer or camán matches in the *Derry Journal* or *Donegal Independent* of 1884 (although there is oral evidence recorded in the Burt and Ardara club histories that camán matches were played between townlands in their respective areas at the time). Instead, there are reports at this time on the Donegal regatta, horse racing and even a walking race. Regattas appear to have been important social events around the coast and there are claims that these date back as far as 1740 in one area of Donegal.[44] Athletic sports were held annually in some villages around the county before the first association football and rugby clubs were set up in the second half of the 1880s. The growth in popularity of team games such as cricket and association football in Donegal in favour of these individual sports at the beginning of the 1890s is not dissimilar to the trend noted by Mike Huggins in his study of soccer in north-east England between 1876 and 1890.[45]

The sinking of the gunboat HMS *Wasp* with the loss of fifty lives off the coast of Tory Island on the morning of 22 September 1884, while the crew were on their way to help carry out evictions on the island of Innistrahull at the mouth of Lough Foyle, dominated the local news in the months prior to the founding of the GAA on 1 November 1884.[46] There is no mention in those newspapers of that famous meeting led by Michael Cusack in the Billiard Room of Hayes Commercial Hotel on the first day of winter that year. Clearly, the foundation of the GAA did not receive much attention in Donegal at this time and it was another twenty-one years before any county committee for organising GAA matches was formed. According to Pádraig

S. Mac a' Ghoill, 'this awakening was too slow to become effective in the Northern counties of Ireland'.[47] Donegal's isolation from these GAA affairs meant that it would be Christmas 1886 before the press would report on any attempts to instigate codified Gaelic games in the county. Firstly, the state of the county around this time will be looked at briefly.

COMMUNICATIONS AND TRANSPORT

The poor communication network in the county was illustrated by P.T. McGinley in a letter published in the *Derry Journal* in October 1886. He highlighted the need for the communication and transport network to be developed when he wrote:

> Until this county is opened up by railways and telegraphs, its resources cannot be known, nor can its industrious people get a fair field for their labours. The fishing industry is handicapped, the mineral wealth of the county blocked up, and the traffic impeded for want of railways and telegraphs.[48]

That same week, in another letter highlighting the inadequate telegraph system which was written by 'A Sufferer' living in Ballybofey, it was claimed that, 'there is no telegraph station between Dunfanaghy and Glenties, a distance around the coast of about seventy or eighty miles'.[49] Donegal was described in 1884 as comprising of 'an area of 1,1197,154 acres, of which 231,488 are under tillage, 380,510 in pasture, 7,517 in plantations, 554,759 waste, bog, mountain', with a further 22,880 acres under water.[50] East Donegal was served by the Finn Valley Railway lines from Strabane (Tyrone) to Stranorlar, Derry to Buncrana and from Enniskillen (Fermanagh) to Bundoran in the south.[51] This company had been established by a number of businessmen and landowners from the Finn Valley area in 1863, and in 1882 the West Donegal Railway Company was formed, although the line from Ballybofey did not reach Donegal Town until a new station was built in 1889.[52]

Inishowen and the north-west were linked by the Letterkenny and Lough Swilly Railway, while the County Donegal Railway reached Killybegs in the south-west in 1893 and the more southerly town of Ballyshannon in 1905.[53] However, these rails lines did not cover all areas, and the transport system at the time was frequently lamented in the local press, with the poor condition of the roads also being condemned. This state of affairs will later be addressed for its influence on the development of local sport. The mountainous landscape and underdeveloped infrastructure did little to help the development of the GAA at the time, and it was not until 1888 that the first teams from Donegal were competing in any type of organised GAA competition, with a small number of Inishowen teams taking up the challenge of their Derry neighbours.

CHANGES IN DONEGAL SOCIETY

According to Alvin Jackson, Michael Cusack was 'actively impressed by the dangers of British cultural domination, of what he called in his opening manifesto, published in October 1884, "the tyranny of imported and enforced customs and manners" and of "foreign and hostile laws and the pernicious influence of a hitherto dominant race".[54] The Clare schoolteacher 'advocated the resurrection or propagation of the ancient traditions of the country, and in particular hurling and athletics'.[55] This view of Cusack's was fundamental to his involvement in his founding of the GAA. Mike Cronin believes that 'the 1880s were a highpoint in the organisation of Irish nationalist politics and culture'.[56] He also feels that 'in the wake of the dislocation that the famine caused, a new breed of Irish intellectual emerged who was not content to allow Ireland to continue its existence within the Union'.[57] Although John Tunney believes that it is hard to define 'the dominant position that Protestants continued to enjoy for most of the nineteenth century as a hangover from the earlier era', he is of the opinion that, 'certainly in a county such as Donegal, while the ascendancy *per se* may have gone, it continued to exist insofar as the minority controlled almost every aspect of life in the community'.[58]

The political situation in Donegal in the latter half of the nineteenth century was dominated by Tories and Liberals, who were part of the landed gentry, and the Church of Ireland. Men such as Thomas Connolly and the Marquis of Donegal, who were both elected to Westminster to represent the county in 1868, had a strong grip on social affairs and as well as being landowners, 'acted as magistrates, were members of grand juries, as well as boards of guardians and often presided over local societies and organisations'.[59] Connolly died in 1876, and Marquis Hamilton was defeated in the general election of 1880 as the Liberals came to power, but in the years between 1880 and 1885 this support for the Liberal and Tory parties began to go into decline. Tunney believes that:

> Donegal had begun to show signs of a growing popular nationalism since the mid-1870s. This explains, for example, the large and enthusiastic St Patrick's Day demonstration that occurred in 1877 and which continued in the years that followed. The militant turn that the Land War took in 1884, particularly in west Donegal, led Catholics to insist that their demands be presented with greater vehemence and by public representatives who actually shared them. The jailing of Fr. McFadden of Gweedore and the subsequent unwise use of coercion by the authorities politicised many priests.[60]

This in turn meant that priests played a significant part in the registration of voters for the General Election of 1885, which saw the Irish Parliamentary Party win three seats, 'with a crushing display of political muscle-flexing by Donegal's Catholic majority'[61] Fr McFadden would later provide a strong voice in the Gaelic revival in Donegal at the beginning of the twentieth century and he became heavily involved in the GAA's attempt to eradicate the playing of 'foreign sports'. The Local Government of Ireland Act of 1898 was intended 'to make local government more democratic' and 'within twenty years the total control that Protestants had enjoyed over the county's local and parliamentary politics had disappeared'.[62] Donegal society underwent what Tunney describes as a 'remarkable transformation' in the years between the Great Famine and the Great War, and 'slowly, but relentlessly, Catholics began to replace Protestants as the influential and dominant faction in society'.[63] In any case, events such as the Land War would have been disruptive to the development of Gaelic games in Donegal society, as energy would have been directed elsewhere.

EARLY FORMS OF FOOTBALL AND STICK-AND-BALL GAMES

It is difficult to establish when exactly football and stick-and-ball games were first played in the county, although there is clear evidence of a variation of hurling on a fifteenth-century grave slab at Clonca near Carndonagh.[64] However, while a stick-and-ball game, known variously as *iomáin*, hurling, or 'common' (from camán) has been present in Ireland since at least the seventh century, Eoin Kinsella believes that 'it is not possible to definitely trace the development of the game up to the late nineteenth century'.[65] The most significant evidence of early forms of hurling in Donegal lies in a number of interviews conducted by Seán Ó hEochaidh in 1943 and this has been well documented by Liam P.

Ó Caithnia in *Scéal na hIomana.*[66] P.S. Mac a' Ghoill has also recorded evidence of cross-country hurling in Donegal and this will be addressed later.[67]

Variations of soccer, Gaelic football and hurling may have been played in various communities prior to the codification of these sports in Ireland, but, as Hugh Dan McLennan has noted in his work on shinty, there have been many variations of ball-and-stick games played throughout the centuries and 'all reveal an unmistakable community of origin' but it is extremely difficult to establish when exactly 'any one emerged from the parent stem and acquired a distinct form and individual existence'.[68] This means that, as Mike Cronin has stated, 'caution should be practiced before these games are given the name hurling and linkages made between past and present'[69], as has been the case in the works of a number of GAA writers.

The same could be said of Gaelic football; there were many forms of ball games in various cultures, and Cronin believes that 'Ireland shared, along with many other nations, a history of a mass ball game. In Britain, and elsewhere in Europe, this is identified as folk-football, a game which, when codified, becomes association football or soccer.'[70] This 'mob-style game' involved 'large groups of men trying to propel a ball in one direction or another towards a goal. The game would have been chaotic, rule free, and involving massive numbers of men.' Cronin therefore states that Gaelic football 'is not a game of clear origins with national characteristics and a long history, it is part of the late-nineteenth-century obsession with rules and organisation'.[71]

THE POPULARITY OF CAMÁN IN DONEGAL

It is also apparent that the sport of camán was more popular than Gaelic football in the country in the early years of the Gaelic Athletic Association. Neal Garnham believes that, 'for sportsmen eager to take up a game that had the image of the Irish hero more closely attached to it, hurling was the obvious choice'.[72] There were many initial problems with the rules of Gaelic football which needed to be clarified and of course the sport also faced stiff competition from rugby and soccer. Significant rule changes did take place in the 1890s, at the instigation of Richard Blake, Chairman of the Meath GAA, which helped make the sport more appealing for both players and spectators, but it was not until the middle part of the first decade of the twentieth century that 'popular interest in the game as a spectator sport was finally being aroused'.[73] This progress was undoubtedly helped by changes in the GAA's administrative personnel at the start of the twentieth century, along with the foundation of provincial councils in 1901. The ban on players participating in rugby or soccer, which had been reinstated in the same year, was to become a permanent fixture in 1905.[74] This, however, proved almost impossible to implement in Donegal at this time and the problems encountered by those trying to curtail the popularity of soccer and promote an adherence to the playing of Gaelic games only will be looked at in chapters three and four.

The popularity of and participation in the sport of camán throughout Donegal at this stage can be seen in the problems encountered by the Donegal county board in selecting a county Gaelic football team at their meeting prior to St Patrick's Day, 1906. The majority of clubs who replied to the offer of sending players for the Donegal team to face Derry on St Patrick's Day, 'could not see their way to send any members, as they had been engaged all the time to the camán, and had given no attention to Gaelic football. The Gweedore team was a notable exception.'[75] Therefore, the Donegal selection, which was beaten by Derry in the Ulster football championship of 1906, was made up mainly of players from Gweedore. Others who turned up were from Newtowncunningham, Burt, Fahan, Glenties, and Bundoran. Unsurprisingly, the team suffered from a lack of collective practice and tactics were largely non-existent, with players criticised for their lack of co-operation.[76]

IMPROVEMENTS IN GAELIC FOOTBALL

Australian sports historian W.F. Mandle has written that:

> Gaelic football, like all pre-codified folk football in the nineteenth century, would be, to the modern eye, an unstructured shambles. It was a rough-and-tumble game in which wrestling and tripping were allowed. Even the first Gaelic football rules allowed individual wrestling to occur whilst the game proceeded … style and tactics were geared to close, rushed ground play, there was much fly-kicking and little catching.[77]

Improvements in the scoring system and the development of a parallelogram, which reduced congestion in front of goal, along with a more efficient passing system emphasised by Kerry and Kildare, and 'ground foot-passing in soccer style' by the northern counties all helped to make Gaelic football more attractive by 1914.[78] Hurling also benefited from the use of more open play, and in the early 1900s the use of both lighter hurleys and balls were advantageous to the game's development.[79] Mandle claims that, 'in effect Gaelic games were doing, ten or fifteen years later, what soccer and rugby had been doing in Britain in the closing decades of the nineteenth century'.[80] With the popularity of association football in Donegal, it was not until 1906 that a competitive structure for Gaelic football was set up.

EARLY FORMS OF HURLING IN DONEGAL

It is clear that camán matches took place between townlands long before the founding of the county board in 1905 and this has been documented in the Burt, Kilcar and Ardara clubs' history books.[81] Hurling was certainly being played along the west coast of Donegal in Gortahork, Ardara, Glencolmcille, Kilcar, Inver, Donegal Town, Ballyshannon and Bundoran, while it was also noted on Inishboffin, Fahan and at Burt in the Inishowen peninsula in the years prior to the founding of the GAA. There were two main types of hurling played: 'commons' was played on a restricted field and the other type, cross-country hurling, took place across townlands.[82] In north-west Donegal, cross-country hurling was played on the island of Inishboff in the second half of the nineteenth century, and the islanders, 'as fast as hounds', apparently were unbeaten in their games against those from the mainland until the sport died out.[83]

In the parish of Cloughaneely it was traditional for ground hurling to be played between townlands until nightfall on Christmas Day, after a drop of poitín had been taken. The object of the game was to keep the 'cnag' or wooden ball in their own townland and bring it back from the place which they had originally left. Games would begin after dinner, with an old person from the locality throwing in the ball. One side having won possession, a fast pursuit would then take place, sometimes in heavy snow, often over ditches, heights and rivers. Teams were also formed for games on a restricted area, with goal scoring the aim. Hand and finger injuries were commonplace and players would at times swim up to their necks to secure the 'cnag'. In those days, travel from other parishes such as Dunfanaghy was extremely difficult over the mountainous terrain and the short hours of daylight on Christmas Day would have rendered such a journey impractical. This Christmas Day tradition is thought to date back to 1750 at least and it was not until the Great Famine, with the social dislocation, deaths and emigration it brought, that the locals lost their enthusiasm for these games.[84]

These forms of sport were not restricted to Donegal of course. Seamus J. King has discussed the development of these variations of hurling in his book *A History of Hurling*. He also states that camán or 'commons' was a winter sport played on a confined area, and 'it resembled hockey or the Scottish game of shinty in that it used a thin crooked stick and a hard ball and was played solely with the stick. This was the game in the north of the country and of the common people.'[85] Iomáin or báire, which was played in the summer, was the other variation of hurling. It was played with 'what would now be regarded as a typical hurley stick, the broad camán, and a softer ball of hair that might be lifted by the hand to be struck with the stick. The game needed a large area and might be played across country.'[86] The standard set of rules drawn up by Maurice Davin, and unveiled by him at the third meeting of the GAA on 18 January 1885, were more similar to the southern game of báire and this meant that camán went into decline in many areas, particularly in Ulster, although it survived for a short while in Donegal. Significantly, King believes that the most successful hurling counties today are from the báire area.[87]

REGIONAL VARIATIONS

According to Mac a' Ghoill, there were distinct variations between the way 'commons' was played in north Donegal and in the south of the county, 'The Burt hurley with the narrow boss and ridge along the heel was peculiar to north Donegal, while the wider boss with ridge was used in the southern half of the county where the broad boss hurley with hollow for carrying was used by forwards.'[88] This type of hurl 'was probably used in cross-country hurling in south-west Donegal in the early years of the century'[89] This game was popular in Ardara and was played with a 'bool' made of 'briar-root, rounded under the embers of the turf fire until it was round and hard on the outside'.[90] Weighing half a pound or more, this type of ball was three inches in diameter and would generally last up to two months.[91] In one match the playing field covered a distance of five miles, from Glengesh to Kilraine, and the famous Glengesh Pass was the setting for games between teams from Glengesh and the nearby Scadaman area between 1897 and 1906.[92] Of the seventeen players named by Mac a' Ghoill from the Glengesh team which took part against their Scadaman rivals in 1899, it is possible to establish the occupations of twelve of these. Unsurprisingly, the majority were involved in agriculture, with children as young as nine years old taking part; three sets of brothers can be identified – the Breslins, McHughs and McGills.[93]

THE DECLINE OF CROSS-COUNTRY HURLING

Cross-country hurling seemed to go into decline after the founding of the GAA county board in 1905, as the rules of báire became more commonly implemented. With the codification of hurling after the foundation of the GAA, camán matches on a restricted field with a set number of players became implemented and gradually evolved to the rules which are more familiar nowadays. Goals and points were registered, and initially, points were also scored for striking the ball outside of the goalposts between two additional posts situated twenty-one feet to the left and right of the goalframe. These outside posts were not removed until 1910. A goal was also worth more than any number of points scored until this was changed to equal five points in 1892 then three points in 1896. The number of players, which was originally listed as a maximum of twenty-one on each team, was lessened, and changes were also made in the size of the playing field.[94]

The Glengesh Pass.
(Courtesy of Jessica Nehf)

THE SUCCESS OF BURT

Ardaghey were defeated by Burt in the 1906 Donegal championship final for the Bishop's trophy at the Aonach in Letterkenny in July 1906.[95] (This competition will be looked at in more detail in chapter three.) Burt went on to represent Donegal and were victorious in the Ulster final, which was played, as was often common in those days, much later, in July 1907.[96] King also believes that the reasons for the success of Burt in these early years lies in the fact that they adapted more effectively to the Munster game of hurling and it is clear that were much more efficient at the sport than their counterparts from southern Donegal – a trait which continues to this day. Speaking in 2000, *Derry Journal* editor Pat McArt claimed that the reason for Burt's strong tradition of Gaelic games throughout the twentieth century lies in the fact that the parish is close to Derry, and 'the volatile nature of the political scene there kept alive in Burt a keen awareness of all things Irish, and hurling and football were very much part of that culture.'[97]

Mac a' Ghoill believes that emigration, the Great War and the War of Independence also meant that local competitions in south Donegal and the playing of camán in Donegal went into decline after 1909.[98] There are now no senior hurling clubs in the north-west or south-west divisional areas of Donegal, and in 2009 the only clubs with hurling teams were Aodh Ruadh (Ballyshannon), Buncrana, Burt, Carndonagh, Four Masters (Donegal Town), Sean MacCuamhaills (Ballybofey), Setanta (Killygordon) and St Eunans (Letterkenny).[99] However, a number of the initial GAA clubs in Donegal in the period from 1888–1892 were primarily engaged in hurling.

INITIAL ATTEMPTS TO ORGANISE THE GAA IN DONEGAL

In a letter to the *Derry Journal* written on 13 April 1886, 'Harp', a Dublin-based Gael, questioned the lack of GAA activity in the north of the country. He claimed that he could not 'understand why the north should be behind the rest of Ireland, when a work of such importance is going on'.[100] He highlighted the success of a number of northern 'athletes' in the Cusack-founded Metropolitan hurling club in Dublin, one of these being a young man named C.J. McGarvey from Rathmullan.[101] McGarvey made a return to his native parish the following Christmas and, having taken part in the local concert and dramatical entertainment at the Courthouse on 20 December,[102] was instrumental in organising a fourteen-a-side hurling match in a field loaned by Mr Batt, which took place on Christmas Day.[103] Despite the fact that the young men played with a mixture of hurleys and 'crooked sticks called *camáns*', the game was 'thoroughly well contested and lasted for upwards an hour'.[104] D. McGrorey's team defeated McGarvey's by two goals to nil and another match was fixed for New Year's Day, but the sport did not develop in the town without the leadership of the Metropolitan club player who seemingly returned to the capital after his Christmas break.[105]

It is apparent that a number of sporting events took place only during holiday times and traditional dates, but this is the last reference to hurling in Rathmullan in the local press around this time.

THE FIRST DONEGAL GAA CLUBS

Burt Hibernians GAA club was formed on 5 February 1888 with the help of visitors, St Patrick's GAA club, Derry. The teams participated in a hurling match at Molaney, Burt, using, in the first half, Burt's traditional camán rules and those of the GAA in the second period.[106] Burt played the match barefooted and their 'nag' or wooden ball was used in the first half while a leather ball was introduced for the second. The game was played without sidelines and it appears that Burt were the winners.[107] Interviews with prominent Burt goalkeeper Jamie McLaughlin, who starred on their team in the early 1990s, suggests that a form of hurling had been played in the area around the time of the Great Famine.[108] At Christmas 1888 they became the first Donegal hurling team to compete in a tournament organised by the GAA in Derry.[109]

At the Derry GAA County Convention on 28 October 1888, Burt were the only Donegal team represented,[110] but other areas in Inishowen were also expressing an interest in Gaelic games. On Sunday 18 November, St Columb's of Derry travelled to Buncrana to help organise a club there. After a match in which the Derry men were joined by 'the stalwart sons of Inishowen' a meeting was held by 'the young men of Buncrana' and the Cahir O's GAA club was formed there.[111] This club name was in memory of Sir Cahir O'Doherty, Lord of Inishowen, who was killed by Crown forces near Kilmacrennan on 5 July 1608, having sacked and burned Derry City.[112] These GAA clubs were clearly eager to illustrate their nationalist allegiances through choice of names. Despite the influence of the Irish Republican Brotherhood in the GAA at the time, it is difficult to trace the exact amount of the secret society's involvement in the early Donegal GAA clubs. This club was chaired by D. Doherty, and at a meeting held before Christmas 1888, treasurer John Hagan reported on the subscriptions he had received before 'a very large attendance of the members'.[113]

COMPETITIVE MATCHES

Burt Hibernians, wearing orange and green, were the only Donegal club to take part in the Derry hurling championship of 1889. Despite winning their first match against St Columb's of Derry in January,[114] they were defeated at the semi-final stage by Derry side Young Irelands, in a game described as 'the only real exhibition of hurling since the formation of the Gaelic [association] in Derry'.[115] Burt had been tipped to win as they were the 'heavier' team, but 'the careful passing of the ball by the Young Irelands entirely outwitted them'.[116] Later that year, it was claimed in the *Derry Journal* that the 'camán' used by the Burt team was to blame for the heavy defeat, 'as it is impossible for it to cope with the hurley either when the ball is on the ground or in the air'.[117] Cahir O's continued to play Derry teams in both Gaelic football and hurling matches throughout 1889, as the train line into the town provided a convenient means of travel, and they had some notable victories. On Sunday 4 August they challenged Derry champions, Hibernians on their home ground beside the Swilly. Despite being described as a 'hard nut to crack', the 'sturdy Cahirs' were well beaten before a large crowd in both matches.[118] Clubs would often play back-to-back hurling and Gaelic football matches on the same day, with the visitors being entertained in a local hotel or public house in the evening.

THE FIRST DONEGAL GAA SELECTION

A new county committee was formed in Derry in November 1889[119] but, surprisingly, Burt did not take part in the Gaelic Athletic tournament held at Springtown that Christmas. It appears they were not affiliated with the new county board and Donegal was represented only by Killea Hibernians (green and yellow) and Portlough Harps (green and red), who played for a silver medal on Christmas Day. It was reported that, 'although both clubs have only recently started ... a first-rate hurling match was witnessed'.[120] Unfortunately, little else has been recorded about their origins. These two clubs were joined by Cahir O's for an eighteen-a-side hurling match against a Derry selection the same day. Donegal, wearing green jerseys and captained by James Harkin from Buncrana, were trounced by their opponents and without their reputable Burt compatriots this was no great surprise.[121]

At the beginning of 1890, Newtowncunningham Harps were becoming involved in challenge matches, and after one of these, in January against McCarthy's of Derry, it was reported that, 'the Harps, although quite a young club, made splendid play in both matches'.[122] In April, 'Referee' chartered the progress the Newtowncunningham club had made:

> The Newtown men since their establishment have let no grass grow under their feet. Twenty-one suits of uniform were purchased last week, and, besides a splendid stock of hurleys, the treasurer still has a surplus of £10 in his till. The Newtowns have set an example which it would be well for some of the city clubs to follow.[123]

By September it was noted that, despite the disarray of the Derry County Committee, Newtown were still in training, while Killea Hibernians were 'at present disbanded'.[124] Buncrana had two GAA clubs around this time, Emmets and Cahir O's, although the former was the only one mentioned along with Burt Hibernians and Newtown at the County Convention to reorganise the GAA in Derry at the end of September 1890.[125] It was reported at the GAA's Annual Convention that Derry and Donegal had sixteen affiliated clubs between them, while Galway led the way with sixty-three. It was also estimated that there were 263 clubs located in Leinster, 137 in Munster and 87 in Connacht, while Ulster had only 37.[126]

The Derry committee managed to organise a number of tournaments towards the end of the year, and Burt were strongly favoured to reach the final of the County Derry Hurling Challenge Cup the following March, having defeated Newtown in the first round.[127] They faced Derry club Bright Stars in the second round on Easter Monday, but, like Donegal rivals Newtown, who faced St Patrick's (Waterside) in the Gaelic football competition, they were defeated.[128] With the Parnell Split and the decline of the GAA in Derry around this time, there is little mention of Donegal clubs' activities until August 1892.

THE DECLINE OF THE GAA IN THE 1890S

In April 1892, it was reported that, 'it is a fact that not in Derry alone, but in other parts of Ireland, the Gaelic Athletic Association is in decline'.[129] This was a reference to the Parnell Split, and many GAA clubs splintered over support for Charles Stewart Parnell after he was rejected as leader of the Irish Party following his affair with Kitty O'Shea. According to Damian Dowds, 'the Bishop of Derry had come out strongly against Sunday games and this had affected the organisation greatly in the area'.[130] Con Short believes that Gaelic games in Ulster had been in decline since the late 1880s and the clergy were largely responsible for this as they frequently came out strongly against Irish Republican Brotherhood involvement in the GAA.[131] By 1892 the Donegal GAA clubs' activities had greatly lessened. On Saturday 13 August 1892, Burt Hibernians took on their Derry namesakes at Rosemount in Derry,[132] but there were no Donegal clubs represented at a meeting of the Derry County Committee on Sunday 14 August.[133] Burt also managed to defeat Derry opposition, cup-holders St Patrick's at a traditional match held on St Stephen's Day[134] but club competitions had ground to a halt in the area and the Burt men would have to wait until 1902 before they could again compete for honours.

However, Dowds believes that this lean decade at the end of the twentieth century was highly significant in the Burt club's history, as 'foundations were laid for greater things to come. Football and hurling was practiced in Burt in preparation for occasional matches, and the club modified their game in accordance with the ever-changing GAA rules.'[135] In January 1893, it was noted in the local press that Newtown and their Derry opposition, Hibernians, 'were much out of practice'[136] but it is notable that the Donegal club were the only others to join Burt in competition when the Donegal organisation was established in 1905. Writing in 1934, former Donegal GAA county board chairman Seán Ó Casaide claimed that 'the irregular configuration and remoteness of the county from the hub of Gaelic activity, as well as the denationalising influences of the guerdon of Imperial forces were contributing causes to the overdue advent into the county of the Gaelic Athletic organisation.'[137]

RIC RECORDS

While acknowledging that, as Mike Cronin has noted, the records of the RIC focused on the GAA mainly for their nationalist links and what they perceived

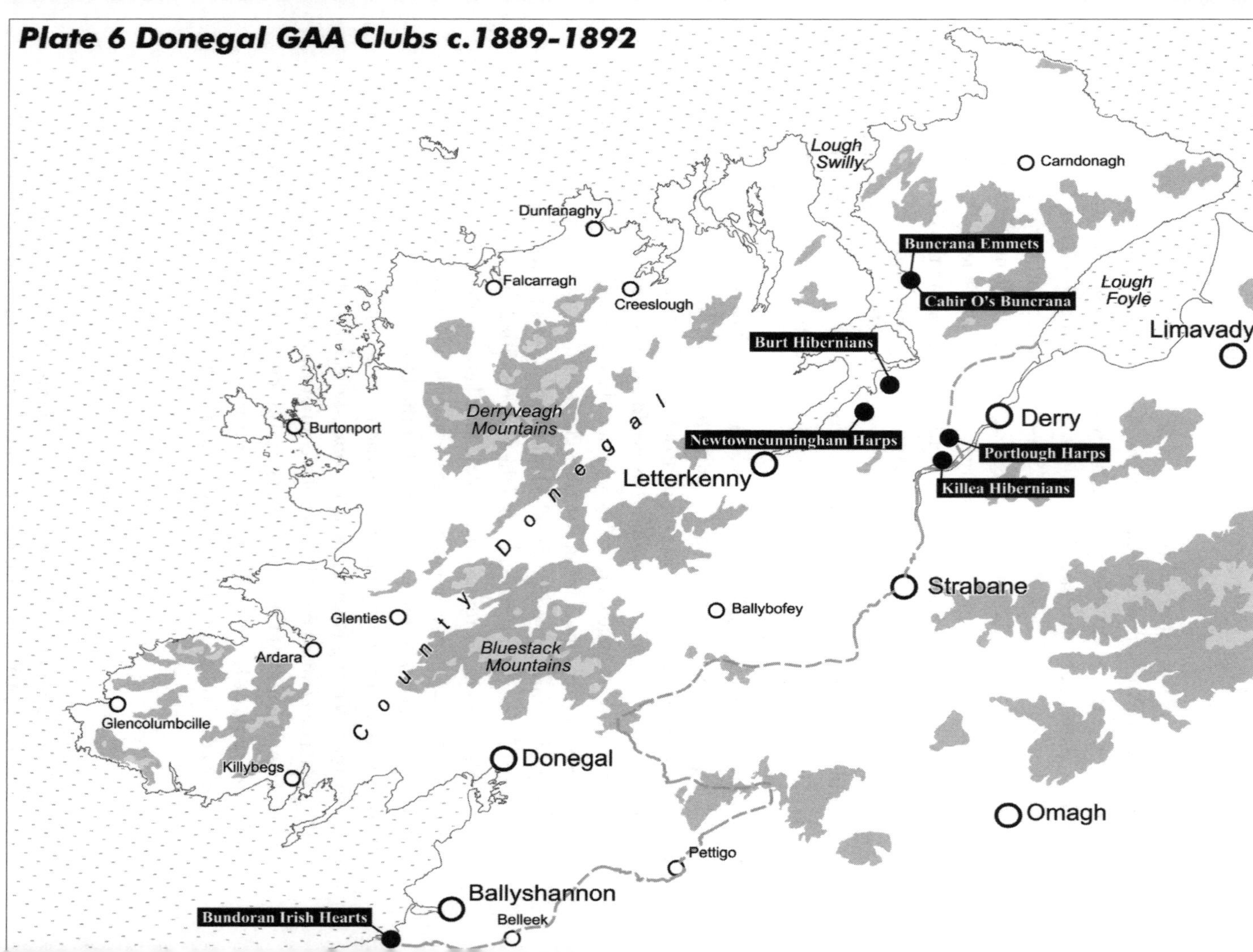

Plate 6 Donegal GAA Clubs c.1889-1892

to be political activities, it is possible to examine the state of Gaelic games in the county to some degree from their records. In 1891, the police force noted that the GAA was 'weakest in Westmeath, Meath, Waterford, Donegal and Armagh'.[138] They also claimed that there were four branches of the GAA in Donegal and that these were all under Fenian control. It was estimated that there were ninety-eight members of these clubs. East Cork had the most branches, with forty-eight, and there were 2,276 members in this area.[139] The 1889 countrywide club figure of 777 dropped to 339 at the end of 1891, but by 1894 the figure was down to 122.[140]

It is clear, then, that there was a significant drop in the number of clubs affiliated throughout the country during the last decade of the nineteenth century, and in fact there were only six affiliated in Ulster in this period, according to Pádraig S. Mac a' Ghoill. He felt that this was 'due no doubt to the Parnell Split and high levels of emigration from the county'.[141] In fact, W.F. Mandle has claimed that 'by the early 1890s the GAA was all but dead'.[142] According to Donal Campbell, 32,410 people left Donegal between 1881 and 1901, and he feels that, 'as the greatest emigration took place among the nationalist population, it is fair to assume that the GAA lost many members'.[143] No Ulster championships were played from 1891 to 1901 and Donegal did not field any teams in these competitions until 1906.[144]

THE BUNDORAN IRISH HEARTS

Although a number of these Inishowen clubs participated both in Gaelic football and hurling, it is hard to establish, without any written records, exactly how much attention, if any, the former received in other areas around the county prior to 1905. A Gaelic football club had been established in the south of the county, in Bundoran, in April 1889 under the name 'Irish Hearts', having been granted permission by James Johnston JP, DL of Kinlough House to use his property for playing purposes. The club felt that this revival of 'ancient Irish games' could 'exercise nothing but salutary effort upon both the minds and bodies of the players, provided they avoid play on Sundays'.[145] They also felt that although their style of play had originally been 'crude … the play became more scientific and lost its wildness'.[146] Their opponents went unrecorded, but it was clear that soccer was more commonly understood and promoted at the time, and it also required less players. In any case, the Bundoran side would have struggled to find opposition within their area of Donegal (see plate 6), and by 1890 the club was taking part in soccer matches.[147]

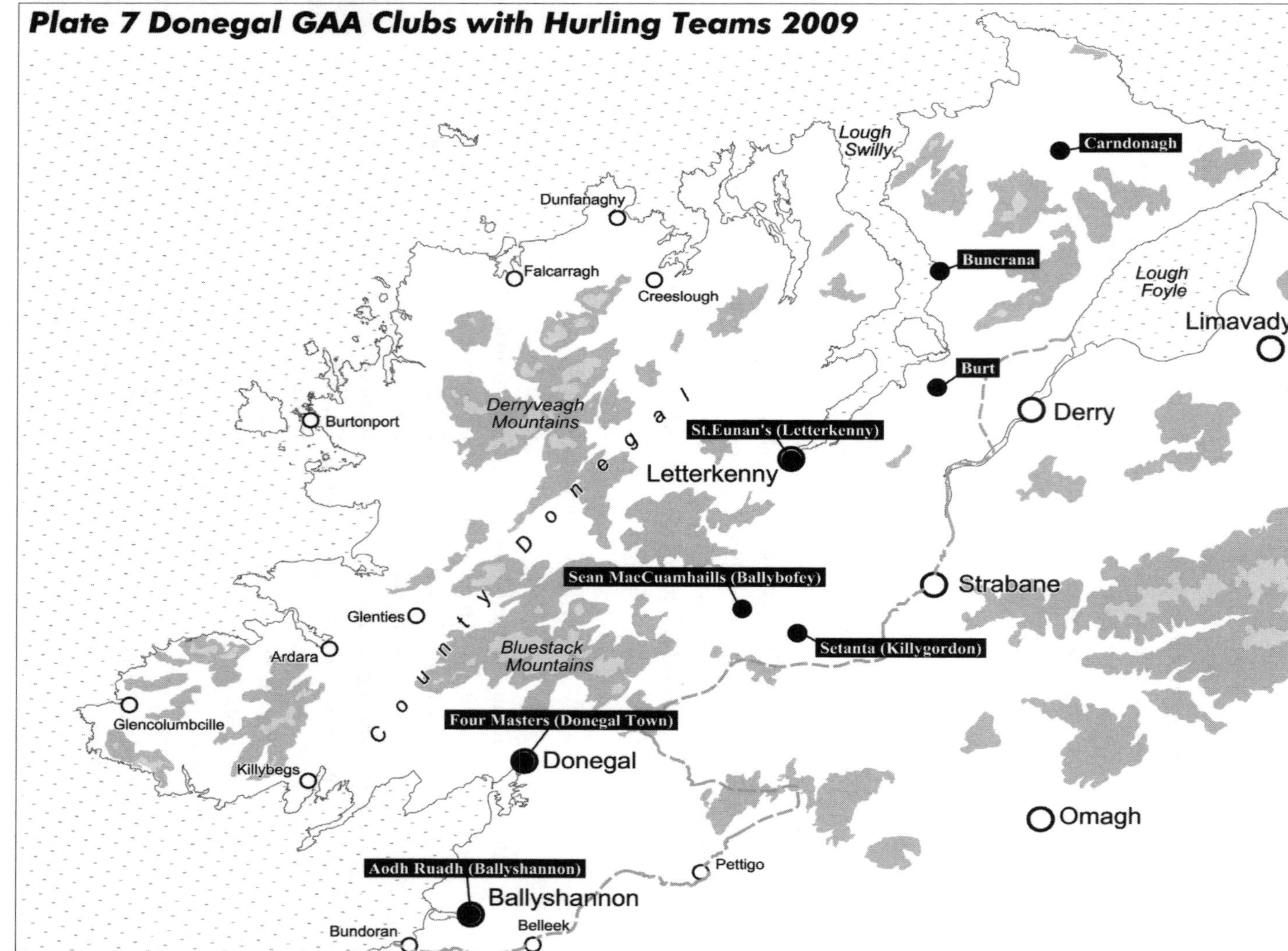

Plate 7 Donegal GAA Clubs with Hurling Teams 2009

CONCLUSION

While there certainly were efforts to promote the playing of Gaelic games in Inishowen at the end of the 1880s and in the early 1890s, the disarray of the Derry county board did little to encourage these clubs' development. The train network which had facilitated their travel to matches was slow to be developed in the county and did not reach all areas. The nationwide decline of Gaelic games that came with the Parnell Split, further stifled any attempts to get the GAA up and running in Donegal. The sheer size and rural nature of the county, with its underdeveloped transport system and poor communications network, also meant that it was impossible for any continuous or widespread development of the GAA in the county at this time.

The poor economic and social conditions which existed, with poverty and famine in certain areas, were contributing factors to the emigration from the county, and a number of factors which, as Cronin has stated, facilitated the sporting revolution in Britain were slow to develop or were completely absent in Donegal. These included a lack of dissemination of sport by past pupils and students of public schools and universities, as the education structure was not the same. Neither was the class system, which saw wealthy industrialists and landowners contribute to the development of working-class sports in England. Allied to this, there were no instigators or leading public figures with the desire, ability or confidence to articulate their views on Gaelic games and promote the organisation in the local press. The early Donegal clubs received little financial backing from would-be patrons, often a crucial factor in the growth of sporting clubs. The Gaelic League did not become prominent in Donegal until the early 1900s, when the nationalist revival was beginning to kick in, and its members' efforts to promote Gaelic games will be addressed later. At the end of the nineteenth century, soccer was the dominant sport in Donegal, and its growth and development will be looked at in the next chapter.

2

ASSOCIATION FOOTBALL IN DONEGAL, 1881-1905

'When the game was started, under the name of the County Donegal Football Association, there was a ringing cheer.'[1]

ASSOCIATION FOOTBALL IN IRELAND

Association football, or soccer, was not introduced into Ireland until October 1878, with an exhibition match between Queen's Park and Caledonians taking place in Belfast. The Irish Football Association was formed two years later, some seventeen years after the English Football Association had been founded.[2] While Alan Bairner and John Sugden have traced soccer's origins in this country to the cross-country game known as 'cad', which was played over 1,000 years ago,[3] Mike Cronin believes that it is hard to say 'whether cad and the other large-scale folk football games are the precursor of what we now understand as soccer, or whether they form the basis of Gaelic football'.[4] Although there is evidence that in the eighteenth century in 'Kerry, Antrim and Donegal entire villages engaged in massive football matches'[5] using animal bladders, it is difficult to establish when exactly the first association football club in the county was formed. However, soccer was certainly being played in the county by 1881.

THE BEGINNING OF ASSOCIATION FOOTBALL IN DONEGAL

Football 'under the association rules' was played between the villages of Castlefin in east Donegal and Croaghan in July of 1881. The game began at four o'clock in a 'best of three' series and continued until half past eight in the evening, 'when it was unanimously agreed to draw owing to the lateness of the evening' despite the fact that Castlefin had scored one goal.[6] It was claimed that 'much interest was manifested on both sides pending the result, and several bets were made, the Croaghan men being almost certain of victory some of their sympathisers [were] giving ten to one on them'.[7] In January 1882, the Letterkenny Athletic Club availed of the generosity of the Hegarty ladies of the local hotel, who granted them their field for 'a well-contested match of football … under association rules.'[8] The match was played between 'the Friendly club' and 'the Town club', although there is little evidence that these teams had a proper administrative structure or were regularly engaged in matches. However, it was noted that this was not the first time that the Letterkenny Athletic Club had availed of the ladies' support. Local man Hugh Gallagher clearly had some knowledge of the rules, as he was put in charge of the match and he was also responsible for conducting the football at the St Patrick's Temperance Guild athletic sports, which were held in August at the same Isle Fields venue.[9] The sports were held under the patronage of the then Bishop of Raphoe, the Most Revd Dr Logue, the Revd Drummond and Fr Sheridan, with prizes being donated by Dr Dunlop and Mr Lydon of the Ulster Bank.[10] The events, which also consisted of foot and novelty races, were also 'open to all classes'.[11]

Football matches were also being played in the south of the county, and during a match between teams representing Mountcharles and Donegal Town in February of 1882, a bad injury was enough to attract the attention of the local press. It was reported that James McLoone, the son of local Justice of the Peace, Mr Joseph McLoone, suffered a broken leg as the result of an accidental kick.[12] The bone was set on the spot by Dr Smith. It would appear that local football in this area needed an incident of this nature, to a prominent young man, to be deemed worthy of note in the local press, as there was little mention of football activity otherwise.[13]

A cricket club had been set up in Ballyshannon in April 1882, and, the season having ended around September, a number of these prominent locals were also involved in the organisation of an association football club in the town for the 1882/3 season.[14] These individuals included the Chairman of the Town Commissioners, Robert Sweeney, solicitor Robert Ross Archer Todd and Dr Atkinson, and it was resolved to play under the rules of the Irish Football Association.[15] There is little evidence that this club participated in any matches after this initial interest, although they did manage to secure a playing field from Mr Hugh Tuthill.[16]

In February 1885, the clubs of Doaghbeg and Rossnakill played a friendly match in Drumnacraig 'on an elegant stretch of sand banks beautifully situated on the western shores of Lough Swilly', located on the property of a 'popular and respected proprietor', Hugh Doherty.[17] This thirteen-a-side unspecified football match lasted for around three hours and it was reported that 'every available foot of vantage ground was occupied'.[18]

The following June, at the annual Cranford athletic sports, Kerrykeel FC defeated Cranford FC in a football match played 'under association rules' in Cranford Park, then the property of the Earl of Leitrim.[19] According to Neil Tranter, 'for upper and middle-class patrons and participants, sport was often a means of either flaunting social status or enhancing popularity and reputation, and, in some cases, even of securing electoral support'.[20] In July 1886, the Kerrykeel club held their well-attended annual athletic sports under the supervision of farmer Patrick George Green, in a field owned by Mr Laird, whom it was claimed, had 'always been most anxious to aid the members of the club'. The well-attended entertainment concluded with 'a general game of football'.[21] Association football appears to have been restricted to local athletic events, which were popular around this time, and sporadic matches, as there were no attempts to form a governing body for soccer in Donegal at this stage.

ASSOCIATION FOOTBALL IN DERRY

The Derry Football Association had been established in April 1886[22] and their competitions would provide valuable experience for a number of clubs in north Donegal in the early years of the next decade. Association football was quickly becoming the most popular sport in the north-east of the county in the 1890s. This was due in no small measure to the area's proximity to the city of Derry and its soccer governing body.

Throughout 1894 there were frequent reports in the *Derry Journal* on the activities of those involved in the North-west Football Association, which had its headquarters in Foyle Street in Derry. The Irish Football Association had been formed in Belfast in 1880 and ten years later there were regional associations in Antrim, Derry and Down, with a Mid-Ulster Association adjudicating over teams from north Armagh and surrounding areas.[23]

Soccer was also growing in popularity in other areas of Donegal in the early 1890s, and it is possible to trace the origins of some of these clubs. In 1891, there

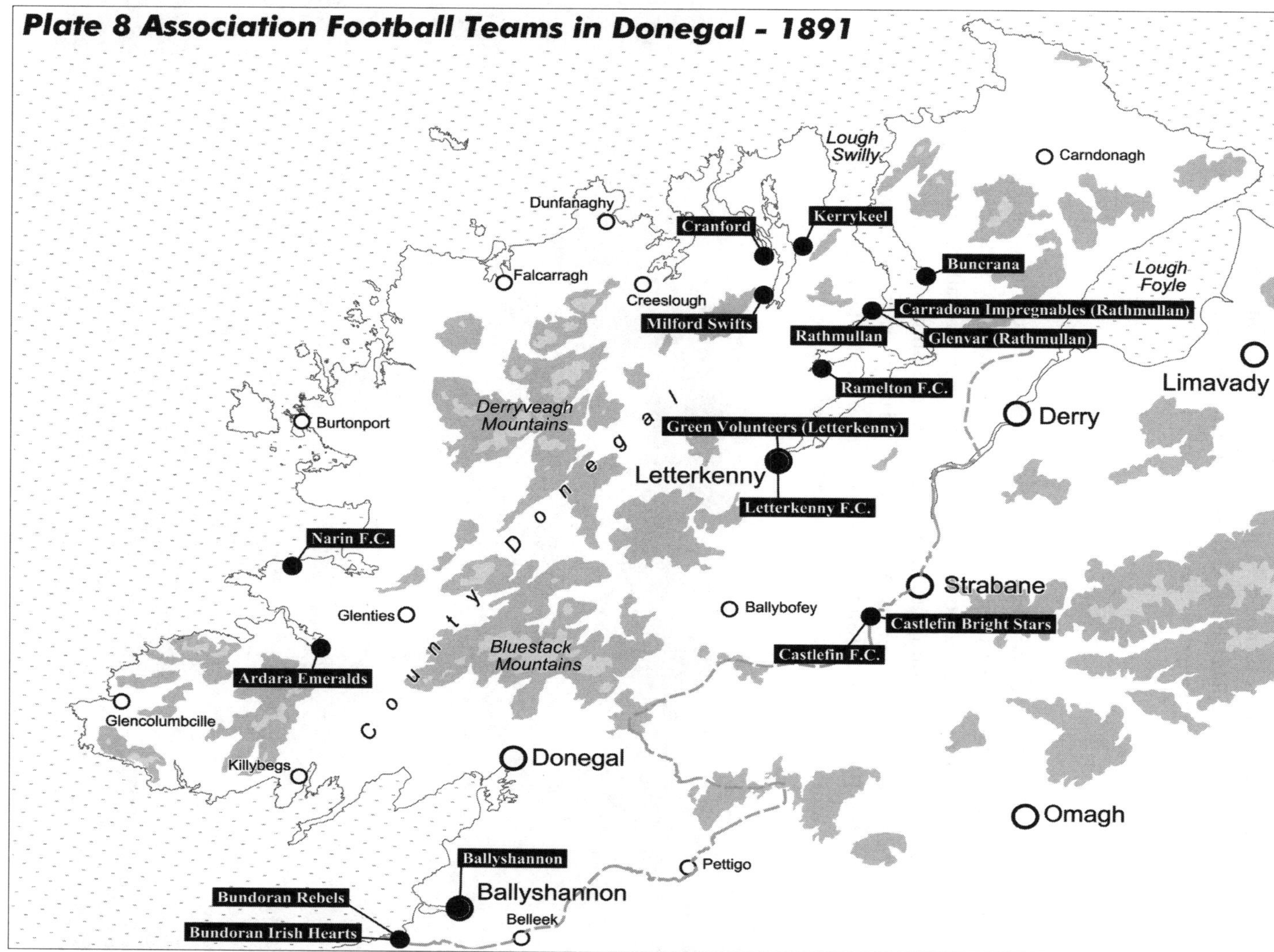
Plate 8 Association Football Teams in Donegal - 1891
Lough Swilly
Carndonagh
Dunfanaghy
Cranford
Kerrykeel
Buncrana
Lough Foyle
Falcarragh
Creeslough
Milford Swifts
Carradoan Impregnables (Rathmullan)
Rathmullan
Glenvar (Rathmullan)
Limavady
Ramelton F.C.
Derryveagh Mountains
Burtonport
Green Volunteers (Letterkenny)
Derry
Letterkenny
Letterkenny F.C.
County Donegal
Narin F.C.
Strabane
Glenties
Ballybofey
Castlefin Bright Stars
Castlefin F.C.
Bluestack Mountains
Ardara Emeralds
Glencolumbcille
Killybegs
Donegal
Omagh
Ballyshannon
Pettigo
Bundoran Rebels
Ballyshannon
Belleek
Bundoran Irish Hearts

were three teams recorded in Rathmullan and two in Bundoran, Castlefin and Letterkenny. Buncrana, Kerrykeel, Milford, Ramelton, Cranford, Ballyshannon, Ardara and Narin were all able to field teams that year.[24]

MUSCULAR CHRISTIANITY

By April 1890, football and cricket practice had been organised in Lifford by Sergeant Major Evans 'for the benefit of militiamen up on training' and it was claimed that, 'hitherto those who did not care for walking had to spend their time either idling at the corners or in the public houses'.[25] This was concurrent with the era of Muscular Christianity, and it was noted that the Ardara Emeralds Football Club in the south-west was founded in April 1891 because of the need to provide some form of athletic club in the town for

Ardara Emeralds FC, *c.*1890–5. (Courtesy of John McConnell)

youths such as shop assistants and apprentices, whom, it was claimed, had 'to spend their leisure hours hanging around the corner'.[26]

PATRONS AND POLITICAL INVOLVEMENT WITHIN CLUBS

There is evidence that some soccer clubs grew out of political organisations. Nearby club 'the Boylagh Champion' was formed in the hall of P.M. Gillespie in Kilclooney on 1 April 1892[27] and a number of men who had significant roles in the Kilclooney branch of the Irish National League were prominent in their football and athletic club's activities, the highlight of these being when they led the local St Patrick's Day procession, which concluded in local man J. Boyle's 'large, level green, consisting of over four acres'.[28] Apparently the thirty members displayed 'remarkable skill and activity for over three hours', before a crowd which had reached 'no less than 500 spectators'.[29] Afterwards, the club members were invited to the hall of former Poor Law Guardian and club treasurer Neil Boyle, where they 'partook of some refreshments and enjoyed a pleasant night close on midnight'.[30] Other association football clubs in the Ardara area at the time included the Cairn Independents and the Ardara Sons of Tyrconnell, but with little coverage of their games in the local press at the time, it is difficult to ascertain how much activity these were involved in.

OUTSIDE INFLUENCE

The development of association football in Donegal was certainly helped by those outside the county. In October 1891, a team representing the County Derry FA was sent to Letterkenny 'to put some interest in the game there'[31] and it was hoped that the match would 'go a great way to developing the game in Donegal'.[32] Later that week, Letterkenny FC received a subscription of £5 from prominent Tyrone politician and linen manufacturer, E.T. Herdman, who had also taken a keen interest in cricket.[33] By April 1893, the Derry soccer body had become the North-west FA and selected an eleven to play a County Donegal team made up of players from Kerrykeel, Letterkenny and Ramelton, in Ramelton.[34] Donegal were victorious on this occasion, and the influence of the Derry men was beginning to pay dividends. In 1893, there were at least thirty soccer teams recorded in the local press, a rise of thirteen from the 1891 figure.[35] However, it must be noted that not all of these clubs had proper administrative structures, and a number of them seemed to have featured only in one-off matches. It is also worth noting that teams such as Milford Swifts, a team said to have replaced the cricket club in the town in 1891,[36] and the Green Volunteers of Letterkenny[37] were occasionally known to use points as well as goals in their scoring system.

The development of the game at that time was also being promoted by visiting ships' crews, who would challenge the locals while in port, and so it is important to look briefly at their influence on Donegal society.

LOUGH SWILLY AND VISITING TEAMS

In a *Derry Journal* article published in September 1893, a brief history of Lough Swilly's fortification was traced, 'Early this century, when the country was under the influence of the French invasion scare, the shores of the lough were hurriedly studded with the forts which still exist.'[38] After inspection in the early 1890s by the commander of forces in Ireland, Lord Wolseley, Prince Louis of Battenberg and a group of engineering and military experts, a scheme was to be put in place which would see the forts at Lenan Head, Dunree, Ned's Point and Inch modernised. It was noted that, 'all the barracks are on the Inishowen side of the lough, the authorities having formed the view that the difficulties of communication on the other side surmounted any advantage that might be gained by remanning Knockalla and Maccamish forts'[39] This development was deemed necessary for strengthening what was perceived to be an inadequate defence of the waterway and to provide shelter for British ships. It was not uncommon for teams from the north of Donegal to take on visiting ships' crews in football matches – in October 1894, Swilly Rangers defeated a team from the HMS *Aurora* in a friendly match.[40] Later that month, Buncrana defeated Royal Engineers by three goals to nil in the same type of match, and it is clear that this element of British culture was particularly enjoyable to many in the area.[41]

While much has been made of the influence of these crews' teams in the promotion of soccer in the Lough Swilly area, it is difficult to establish the exact extent of their activity, the frequency of games, or indeed the standard of their play. These infrequent challenge matches may have attracted local interest at the time, but certainly would not have provided clubs with enough matches to sustain an interest in the game without other local teams' participation throughout the season. There is certainly little evidence that the military in the Lough Swilly area were involved in the formation of any soccer clubs in this area, although a number of these men were later involved in the County Donegal Football Association. While sporting press reports depended upon enthusiasm of club secretaries, there is insufficient press evidence to suggest that ships' crews were playing regularly against local clubs, certainly not in the period covered in this book. Donegal clubs therefore had to look elsewhere for competition.

THE NORTH-WEST JUNIOR CUP, 1894

Throughout 1894 there are frequent reports in the *Derry Journal* on the activities of the Derry, Tyrone and Donegal clubs involved in the North-west Football Association. There were seven north-east Donegal teams affiliated with the North-western organisation at the beginning of 1894: Milford Swifts, Ramelton FC, Ramelton Sunbursts, Carradoan FC, Letterkenny FC, St Adaman's Swifts and Kerrykeel had all registered for the season.[42]

On 10 February, Ramelton took on Milford Swifts in the North-west Football Association Junior Cup for a place in the semi-finals against Omagh Rovers.[43] Milford Swifts were victorious by two goals to nil, but the gulf in class between the Donegal teams and their Derry neighbours became obvious two weeks later at Parkavenue, home of Derry's Northend Milford was trounced by eight goals to three by a strong Omagh side.[44] An illustration of just how far off the top the Milford men were can be seen in the fact that Omagh were outclassed in the final against Clooney Rovers by 5-0 at the Brandywell.[45] However, this semi-final defeat and indeed the Donegal clubs' general lack of success would bring about a turning point in the organisation of soccer in Donegal.

On 9 March 1894, a letter written by Daniel Deeney appeared in the *Derry Journal*. In this letter, Deeney, a former principal teacher in Glenvar NS and honourary secretary of Carradoan FC, a club formed in 1888 and based near Rathmullan, highlighted the Donegal teams' failure to make their mark in the North-west Association's soccer competitions, 'The cup ties of the season, so far as Donegal are concerned, are over, and as usual Donegal has failed to get within pitch-fork length of the prize, or indeed to be very seriously noticed at all. Shall we continue the forlorn competition year after year?'[46] He also suggested that Donegal should form their own association and, in inviting the

Plate 9 The North West Football Association Club Junior Cup 1893-4 Participating Clubs

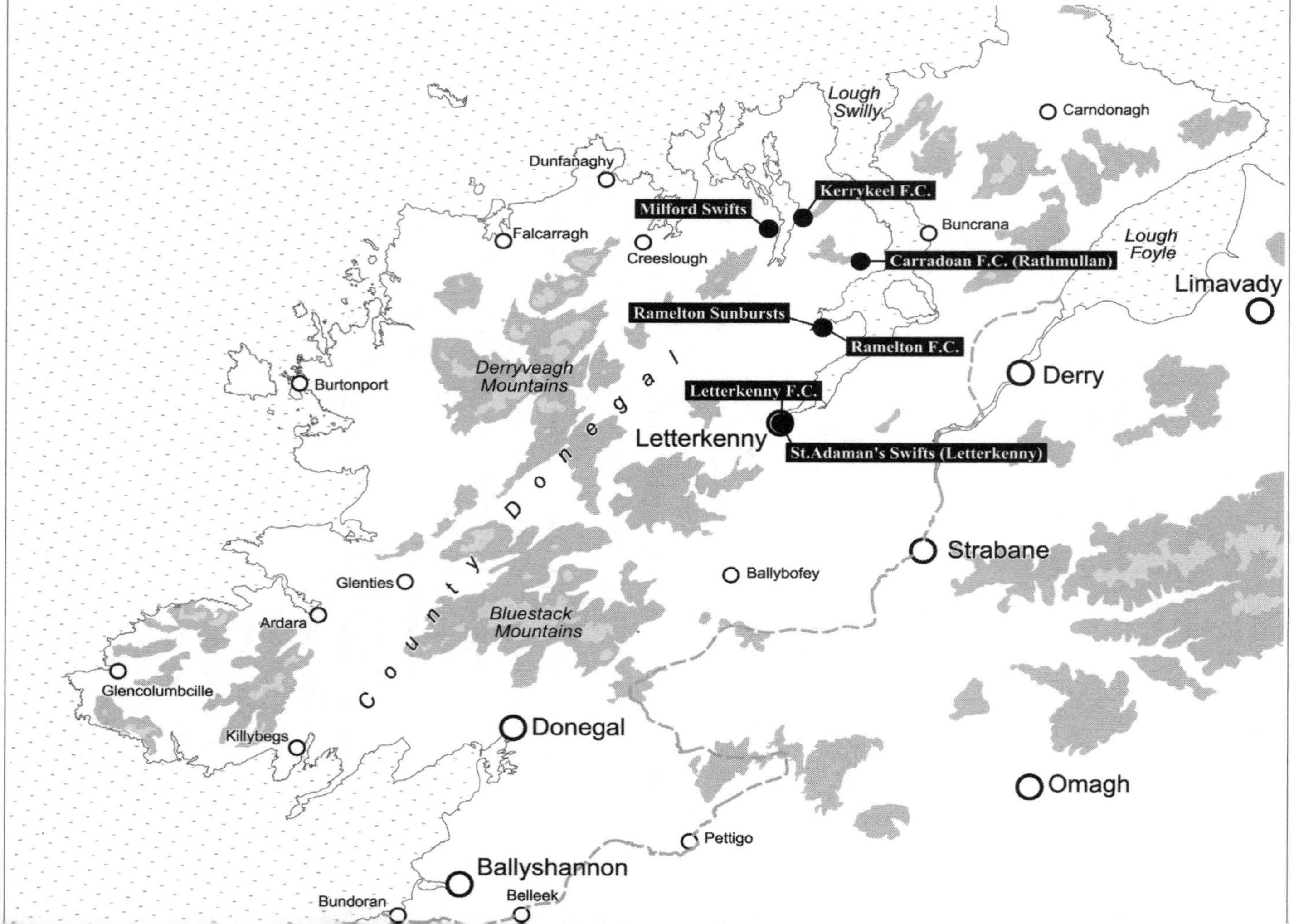

Lough Swilly
Carndonagh
Dunfanaghy
Kerrykeel F.C.
Milford Swifts
Buncrana
Falcarragh
Creeslough
Carradoan F.C. (Rathmullan)
Lough Foyle
Limavady
Ramelton Sunbursts
Ramelton F.C.
Burtonport
Derryveagh Mountains
Derry
Letterkenny F.C.
Letterkenny
St.Adaman's Swifts (Letterkenny)
County Donegal
Strabane
Glenties
Ballybofey
Ardara
Bluestack Mountains
Glencolumbcille
Donegal
Killybegs
Omagh
Pettigo
Ballyshannon
Bundoran
Belleek

secretaries of other clubs to reply to his appeal, he called for a meeting of representatives to take place in Rathmullan on 24 March.[47] He felt that this appeal would reach the many clubs in the county who were not registered with the Derry football organisation, as well as the few who were at this time.[48]

DANIEL DEENEY

Mr Deeney had been instrumental in his local community's entertainment activities, such as literary recital and concerts, and had previous experience of administrative duties, having been secretary and treasurer of his local Vindicator Football Club in 1892 and secretary of the Rathmullan Temperance Association before he returned to St Patrick's College, Drumcondra for additional studies.[49] He was also involved in the Rathmullan Debating Society that year, where he had been appointed treasurer.[50]

His proposal for a new competition was seconded by the secretary of Kerrykeel FC, Patrick George Green, an acquaintance of Deeney's, who wanted to see a cup purchased, and also by Joseph Devenny, secretary of St Adaman's Swifts in Letterkenny, who stated that the majority of Letterkenny footballers were in favour of competing for a Donegal-only cup, 'I think it would be the best and most advisable method of spreading the game in our county. We have had a lot of experience for the past three years, competing for the North-west Junior Cup, and we are as far off as ever.'[51] This new development would also provide non-affiliated clubs in Donegal with a chance to play competitive matches, as friendly matches against local rivals could only help sustain clubs for so long before boredom would set in and clubs would go into decline. A competitive structure within their own county would be of more interest and more practical from a logistical point of view, while the reward of club honours would most certainly be an incentive to those involved.

THE FOUNDATION OF THE COUNTY DONEGAL FA

The founding meeting of the County Donegal Football Association took place in Boyle's Hotel in Ramelton on Saturday 24 March 1894, and Daniel Deeney took the chair.[52] Eight clubs, all from the north-east of the county, were represented: Ramelton, Ramelton Sunbursts, Cranford, Cratlagh (Milford), Milford Swifts, Kerrykeel, Letterkenny and Carradoan. An executive committee was formed and the main proposals were discussed – it was agreed to sever links with the Derry football organisation and the proper means by which to do this were debated. Mr Deeney was appointed secretary and was 'informed to have circulars printed and forwarded to the parliamentary representative for, and the leading gentlemen in, the county soliciting their patronage and support'.[53] Circulars were to be sent to all soccer clubs in Donegal and a benefit match was to be organised, with a team comprising eleven players from the Letterkenny and Ramelton clubs against eleven from Kerrykeel, Milford, Cranford, Cratlagh and Carradoan.[54] It appears that there was no objection from the North-west Football Association to this move and a report on these events appeared in the *Derry Journal* of 30 March, which contained the following sentiments:

> A very important step has been taken by a number of clubs in County Donegal, viz the formation of a football association to embrace all the clubs in that county ... there are a great number of clubs in the county which at present do not belong to any association ... the incentive to join the North-west Association is not strong enough to induce clubs in the remote parts of the county to throw in their lot with other teams more favourably situated, and become members.[55]

It was felt that this new organisation would undoubtedly help non-affiliated clubs who were currently 'playing odd friendly matches' to become involved in a proper competitive structure.[56] The first match to be played under the organisation of the newly formed association took place at the Sunbursts Football Club grounds in Ramelton on the third Saturday in April at 3.30p.m. This exhibition game was well attended, 'There was a large crowd of spectators present, and a resulting good "gate"... When the game was started, under the name of the County Donegal Football Association, there was a ringing cheer.' The Whites (players from Letterkenny and Ramelton) defeated the Pinks (players from Milford, Cranford, Cratlagh, Carradoan and Kerrykeel) by 2-1 and a meeting was held afterwards. Milford Swifts, Cranford, Cratlagh, Kerrykeel, Ramelton, Letterkenny, Letterkenny Celtic, Ards, Clooney Rovers (Derry), Ramelton Sunbursts and Carradoan were all represented and 'it was resolved to affiliate with the Irish Football Association as soon as possible. The secretary and treasurer were empowered to order a cup from Mr Wightman of Derry. The entrance fee for each club was fixed at 5*s*, and the annual subscription at

10*s*.'[57] The decision to affiliate with the Irish Football Association was seen as a wise move by the *Derry Journal*, as it meant that this would 'strengthen the Donegal body in no small measure, and make it of more importance'.[58] It would also give Donegal clubs a chance to participate in their own county's cup and the Irish Junior Cup. The newspaper also urged more clubs to join up 'to strengthen their existence, and become, in fact, truly alive'.[59]

TRANSPORT DIFFICULTIES

There is no mention in the local press of any soccer clubs from the south of the county competing for silverware in 1894. It seems that in any case, transport, distance and finances would have been major problems, and correspondence from 'Cesspayer' to the *Derry Journal* written on 1 March highlighted the need for the condition of the roads in the south of the county to be improved. In a highly critical letter he stated that, 'before the opening of the Donegal and Killybegs Railway, the roads were kept in a pretty fair state of repair, but since then, though the traffic is not near so much, they have deteriorated'.[60] It was clear that the writer was in no doubt about who he felt was responsible:

> The county surveyor or his assistants levies the amount at which each road can be kept in a proper state of repair, and on the day of the sessions each contractor for the several roads hands in his paper with the amount on it at which he is willing to take the road [with the lowest tender usually accepted].[61]

It was therefore the case that contractors couldn't do a proper maintenance job on the road because they weren't getting enough money.

INITIAL CLUBS AND MATCHES

The County Donegal Football Association held its opening meeting for the season in mid-September 1894, and it was agreed that the new competition was to be named the 'County Donegal Challenge Cup'. The draw was made with the following teams being paired: Cranford vs Derrybeg Celtic, Cratlagh vs Ramelton Athletic, Kerrykeel vs Buncrana, and Letterkenny vs Milford Swifts. Swilly Rangers received a bye, and it was agreed that owing to problems with distance and as a reward for their efforts in joining the Association, Derrybeg

Celtic, a club situated in the north-west of the county in Gweedore, would be allowed to play Cranford at Creeslough.[62] It is unclear if the two aforementioned Ramelton clubs had amalgamated, but this may have been the case.

LOCAL RIVALRIES

In September, the organisation was welcomed in the Dublin newspaper *The Sport*, which claimed that 'the north is beginning to wake up'[63], but a report in the *Derry Journal* two months later on a dispute between Buncrana and Swilly Rangers illustrated the problems with administration which existed at the time. This friendly match, which took place on 1 November 1894, was abandoned after spectators entered the field of play having been incensed by the standard of refereeing shown by Mr Deeney. James Farren, secretary of the Swilly Rangers club, later claimed that Buncrana had been playing illegal players from Derry and suggested that some of these men may have been soldiers.[64] While Neal Garnham believes that army involvement was commonplace in association football during this time, and opposition was often provided by military teams when local teams were struggling to find opponents, he also claims that 'military involvement also had it drawbacks for the game'.[65] It was felt by civilians that the soldiers had too much experience at soccer for locals to compete with them; they also had more time for training and could avail of better facilities.[66]

This incident demonstrates how sport can arouse strong parochial feelings and illustrates the local rivalries which prevail between many sporting clubs, indeed this competiveness is an important part of developing local identity for many parishes. The events also highlighted the need for strict adherence to the rules, as the failure by a number of clubs to do so was proving to be a major source of discontent for the newly founded committee.

LOUGH SWILLY RAILWAY INVOLVEMENT

The organisation received a welcome boost at its meeting in Rathmullan on 10 December 1894, when it was announced that the Lough Swilly Railway and Steamboat Company conceded 'the request of the Committee to allow football parties *bona fide* to travel the double journeys for single fares'.[67] This again highlights the difficulties many teams faced with transport at the time and illustrates one of the reasons why the competitions were largely restricted to teams from the north-east of the county, with the exception of the aforementioned Derrybeg Celtic. It is worth noting that local businesses would have benefited from the influx of supporters from away clubs visiting their areas, and reduced fares on train journeys to sporting events and festivals were commonplace at this time.

It was agreed that the establishment of a league would be postponed until the next meeting. Again however, problems with registration of players were noted in the local press when a letter from a Letterkenny Celtic representative was published in which he claimed that their rival Letterkenny club should not be named so, as the players were not from the town and this was certainly a recurring problem for the Donegal FA.[68]

FUNDRAISING AND INITIAL SOCCER TEAMS IN SOUTH DONEGAL

Soccer clubs, in their attempts to raise funds, also provided entertainment for their local communities through musical and dramatic performances, and on Thursday 13 December Swilly Rangers held 'a high class concert' to raise funds in the Courthouse, Rathmullan, which 'was kindly placed at the disposal of the committee by Mr Batt, DL, Rathmullan House'.[69] It was reported that 'there was a record attendance, the [Court]house being literally packed with a most respectable, discriminating, and appreciative audience'.[70] Entertainment was provided by prominent members of the local area, Major Thomas Edmund Batt, JP, William Davis, DI, and Daniel Deeney. There were also performances from Revds W.B. Lloyd and Edward Lombard. A number of ladies sang and played the piano and the hornpipe was danced by two 'youthful performers'.[71]

A number of Donegal teams not affiliated with the organisation took part in friendly matches over the Christmas period. Milford Celtic, Lifford and Lifford Young Bloods all managed to field teams, and it appears the Lifford men were committed to the Strabane and Lifford District League around this time.[72] In the south of the county there were teams in Donegal Town and Meenagran (Mountcharles) who met in a series of friendlies on the Hall Strand in Mountcharles. Indeed it was recorded that at a match held there in September 1894 before a crowd of 200, 'one novel feature of the proceedings was, when the tide having encroached a good deal, on the sand, the ball got kicked into the water, and was still played, notwithstanding that the water was up to the knees of the players'.[73]

At this stage the Donegal Town club did not have the means or the playing facilities to join the County Association, but would be one of the first from the area, along with Ardara Emeralds, to be affiliated to the league in 1897.[74] A rugby club had been established in Donegal Town in 1887 under the captaincy of Townsend Gahan, later an inspector for the Congested District Board, and in September 1893 it was proposed 'to conduct the club under both rugby and association rules instead of rugby solely'.[75] However, it is difficult to establish if the aforementioned soccer club had any connection with the rugby organisation.

DISPUTES AND DISQUALIFICATION

The remainder of the 1894/5 soccer season in Donegal was plagued by controversy and protestation. In February of 1895, it was decided to allow teams a thirty-minute grace for lateness and that a 'reasonable excuse' had to be supplied.[76] The County Donegal FA Challenge Cup Final between Derrybeg Celtic and Letterkenny took place on Saturday 20 April 1895 in Kerrykeel. Derrybeg were awarded the cup after Letterkenny refused to continue in the second half, with their opponents leading by a goal to nil. It appears that they refused to play with a new ball after the initial one had burst, 'Only twenty minutes of the second half were played, Letterkenny taking advantage of a temporary cessation of hostilities owing to the ball getting out of order, by leaving the field and refusing to play when a new ball was provided.'[77]

Neither team had won their way through to the final on the pitch. In the semi-finals Ramelton accounted for Letterkenny by 4-1 on Saturday 9 March[78] while Derrybeg had been trounced 5-1 by Buncrana in a match played three weeks later.[79] However, both Ramelton and Buncrana were disqualified from the competition: they both later withdrew from the association, and Ramelton claimed in a letter published on 25 March that Letterkenny had been playing illegal players all season and named three Strabane men, Kane, Harte and Kearney, who had played against them. The two sides played out a 3-3 draw on 16 February, and the replay was arranged for 2 March. Letterkenny refused to travel that day but were soundly beaten the following week. They then lodged a complaint against Ramelton and the protest was upheld. It is not clear why, but the match was ordered to be replayed. At a meeting held on 16 March, president Dr Patterson resigned and advised the Ramelton club to follow him.[80] Buncrana were removed from the competition for fielding two players from the Bright Stars Club in Derry in the semi-final,[81] and it appears that they later took the County Donegal FA to court 'for expenses incurred in conveying their team to Ramelton and Creeslough in the semi-final of the Donegal Challenge Cup', although the result of this appeal went unrecorded.[82]

WITHDRAWAL OF SUPPORT AND THE DONEGAL FA'S DISSATISFACTION

At the Association's Annual General Meeting held in Milford on 18 May, honourary secretary Mr Deeney said he regretted these events but that it had been a learning experience for all involved. Two delegates of the Ramelton club, the Donegal FA chairman, Mr McLaughlin, and Mr McAfee, the honourary treasurer, had earlier resigned their posts, but Mr Deeney said that the eleven meetings had been well attended by the affiliated clubs despite receiving no travel allowances. He outlined the attendance record as follows: Swilly Rangers, eleven; Buncrana and Kerrykeel, ten each; Cranford and Milford Swifts, nine each; Ramelton Athletic and Cratlagh, eight apiece; Derrybeg, five, and Letterkenny, four meetings attended. It was reported that the organisation was in arrears owing to preliminary expenses such as the purchasing of the cup, but the amount to be paid was not a significant figure. Mr Deeney also expressed dissatisfaction with the outcome of the competition, as 'three of the matches were not contested, two of them on account of what were alleged to be unfair decisions of the committee, the other a scratch'.[83] On a more positive note, it was mentioned that there were other clubs eager to join for the 1895/6 season and that 'not one single instance of rough play came under their notice throughout the season'.[84]

DERRYBEG CELTIC FC

The representatives of Derrybeg Celtic were later presented with the cup, and concluded their season on 25 May by playing out a 1-1 draw in a friendly against Cranford. After the match, Fr Mc Fadden of Gweedore illustrated his belief in the temperance movement when he gathered together players and supporters on the pitch. As the nationalist movement grew stronger at the beginning of the twentieth century, he clearly became opposed to association football, but at this point it is evident that he had no problem with the playing of this sport in Donegal provided it was run along temperance lines. He also said that he was 'glad to see from their badges that the Cranford men had joined the temperance movement' and he encouraged other clubs to do so as they would have his support.[85] The difficulties faced by teams who had to travel long distance were also highlighted, 'On the whole the visitors had the worst of the play, but it must be remembered that they were heavily hampered by the long journey and playing so soon after arrival.'[86] Unfortunately these reports in the *Derry Journal* contain little mention of players other than occasional goal scorers and those involved in disputes; it is known that Derrybeg's president was a Mr Breslin and Dr McFadden was also involved in the running of the club.

THE 1895/96 SEASON

At the first meeting of the new season in the Pier Hotel, Rathmullan on 24 September 1895, it was agreed that the league would start immediately, and those at the meeting subscribed to the purchase of a shield from Mr Wightman. Three new teams were allowed to join: Kincasslagh Shamrocks, Letterkenny Celtic and Creeslough. Kincasslagh became the second club from west Donegal to sign up, and the referees for the matches were also appointed.[87] The draw for the Donegal FA Challenge Cup was made in Rathmullan on 15 October and the following teams were paired, with the first named team having choice of venue: Milford Swifts vs Letterkenny Celtic; Cranford vs Creeslough; Swilly Rangers vs Kerrykeel, and holders Derrybeg Celtic vs local rivals Kincasslagh Shamrocks. This meant that along with the aforementioned Buncrana and Ramelton Athletic who had withdrawn, Cratlagh and Letterkenny also declined to take part.

Interest in association football was certainly high in west Donegal as Derrybeg took on Kincasslagh Shamrocks on 9 November, 'before an immense crowd of spectators' in Derrybeg. Kincasslagh were easily defeated by 10-0, which illustrates the difference in class and experience between the two teams at this stage.[88] Kerrykeel refused to play extra time after a one-all draw against Swilly Rangers and were later disqualified after the IFA were asked to intervene. Again the cracks in the implementation of the rules were glaringly obvious.[89] In the semi-finals, which were played on 4 January 1896, Derrybeg accounted for Cranford by 2-0, while Letterkenny Celtic defeated Swilly Rangers by the same scoreline in another match that had been rescheduled after a protest.[90] The final was fixed for 29 February 1896 and Derrybeg Celtic again showed that they were capable of holding their own against opposition from the north of the county. Letterkenny were hammered 5-1 at a rainsoaked Creeslough. There was a large crowd present for a game which went ahead despite fears of postponement, and despite the poor playing conditions. In any case, travel arrangements decreed that the match had to go ahead, 'The weather being unpropitious, the committee of the Association endeavoured to postpone the match, but having been informed by wire that the Derrybeg team had left about eight o'clock on Saturday morning, they decided to allow it to proceed. The ground was rather heavy, owing to rain.'[91]

DANIEL DEENEY RESIGNS

The resignation of the honorary secretary, Daniel Deeney, at a meeting which took place in the Pier Hotel on 25 February, would later have serious repercussions for the Association. Deeney, who had devoted so much of his time to the organisation, announced that he leaving his duties as schoolmaster in Carradoan to take up principalship of a school in Spiddal, County Galway.[92] At a presentation held in the Rathmullan Arms Hotel on Friday 27 February to mark Mr Deeney's Trojan work for the association, he was presented with a valuable inscribed clock of Doric design. The then manager of the Carradoan National School and a good friend of Mr Deeney's, Colonel T.E. Batt made the presentation, and commented that he 'was always to the forefront in everything conducive to the welfare of Rathmullan, and in all branches of amusements and sports'.[93] Colonel Batt also stated that the game 'owed its present position in this part of the county mainly to the able and energetic manner' of Mr Deeney, and it is clear that he was well regarded in their community.[94] The meeting was also attended by other members of the Donegal Football Association, who participated in toasts, recitations and songs, before the evening was brought to a close with the singing of 'Auld Lang Syne'.[95]

1896 AGM

The next AGM of the Donegal FA took place in Rathmullan on 31 May 1896. Milford Swifts were removed from the organisation, 'owing to their refusal to comply with the rules', while Kerrykeel FC left the Association after expressing dissatisfaction with the decision of the country's footballing body that they be disqualified from the cup. Cranford won the league, and Swilly Rangers finished the season as runners-up. The chairman and former schoolmaster, James C. McIntyre outlined the problems that besieged the administration of the county's first football establishment:

> In the discharge of their duties during the season the committee had many difficulties to contend with, chief among them being players and spectators finding fault with the decisions of the referee; disorderly spectators interfering with play and players; the failure of clubs to scratch, and referees to send in the official return within the required time.[96]

FINANCIAL PROBLEMS

The organisation also found itself with a debt of £5 11*s* and 5½*d*. This had come about because:

> … the expenses in connection with starting on a new basis and providing a shield were heavy; the "gates" in the semi-final and final cup ties were insufficient to cover the expenses, which, according to the rules, had to be borne by the association, and the amount of outside subscriptions was very small.[97]

It was hoped that this debt would be cleared by the start of the 1896/7 season and that clubs would organise proper admission fees at cup finals. In relation to this problem it appears that the Donegal FA were not doing a great deal to advertise these finals, with little notice appearing in the local press. Similarly, excursion trains do not appear to have been provided. The choices of Kerrykeel for the 1895 final, and Creeslough for the following season's main event, were, although deemed neutral venues, hardly central locations for cup finals. Events at the time, such as regattas, provided a wider variety of competition, while the annual Cranford Sports also offered more choice of entertainment. There is little in the press reports to illustrate any high level of skill which would make for a better spectacle, and there does not appear to have been any musical bands (often a significant part of a day out's events) organised for the deciding matches. This lack of forward planning did little to raise the profile of soccer in the county, and it is hard to ascertain if the organisation received any financial support from the IFA, or indeed members of parliament, as originally hoped. As Alan Metcalfe has noted in his study of the organisation of soccer in East Northumberland between 1892 and 1914, 'no matter what the level of football, financial considerations determined success or failure' and 'money was a necessary condition for the long-term viability of any club'.[98]

It was also proposed at the AGM that a set of changes in the rules which were drawn up were to be incorporated into the association. The main one was matches being replayed for the worst of disputes. This implementation was later postponed *sine die*.[99] The eight members of the committee were all selected from the Rathmullan district, this being claimed necessary to save representatives of other clubs' travelling expenses. Those chosen were all prominent members of the Rathmullan area, and the committee consisted of: Colonel T.E. Batt, JP; William Davies, DI; Revd Edward Lombard; C.L. Batt; Sergeant Cooley; Mr McCay and James C. McIntyre. There was a significant influence of those in the medical profession in the organisation, with three elected to the positions of office bearers: Dr F. Carre of Letterkenny was elected president, and vice-presidents included Dr M. Loughnan of Rathmullan and Dr McFadden of Gweedore. There was also a notable military involvement with the aforementioned Colonel T.E. Batt, while Major Ker-Fox of Kerrykeel and Lieutenant J.G. Ede of the Royal Navy in Rathmullan were also elected for the coming season. Others elected included: Abraham Manning, a land estate agent living in Mulroy; James Watt Fullerton of Ramelton, a gentleman and farmer, and Milford solicitor John Allan Osborne.[100]

THE 1896/97 SEASON

By the beginning of the new season the outstanding debt had been cleared, thanks to W.E. George of Drumalla House near Rathmullen. He donated £8 of proceeds he had received at an evening of entertainment he had organised for the soccer organisation.[101]

Kerrykeel returned to the Association and were determined to prove themselves. They were joined by two newly affiliated clubs, Castlefin Rangers and Ramelton Polytechnic, while Swilly Rangers were also in the running for league honours. Letterkenny and Buncrana again failed to re-enter clubs. It appears that Derrybeg Celtic did not participate in the league but took the cup again, beating Ramelton Polytechnic by 3-2 in a controversial final on 20 February 1897 at Rathmullan.[102] Kerrykeel won the Rathmullan Presentation Shield for the league, which they received in April.[103]

It was around this time that two teams from the other end of the county began to take more interest in joining their north-east counterparts. Donegal Celtic (south) took on Ardara Emeralds (south-west) on 23 May on Loughrosmore Strand and there was great interest in this friendly contest, 'Long before the hour appointed for the match enormous crowds might be seen wending their way in the direction of the playground, and when the ball was kicked off a great concourse had assembled.'[104] The match finished in a 1-1 draw and they met again in a friendly before another large crowd in September 1897, this time in Donegal Town. Ardara were victorious by 4-0, and these two teams were the first from the south of the county to be affiliated to the league.[105]

THE 1897/8 SEASON

At the beginning of the 1897/8 season the continuation of the league was seriously in doubt. There had been no AGM held at the end of the previous season but by the end of the autumn a new committee had been formed, with Thomas Harity taking over as chairman and Rathmullan saddle and harness maker Thomas Burk Duggan being appointed secretary. Henry Malseed, a farmer, became treasurer.[106] Throughout that winter a number of reports were published in the local press of teams from south Donegal participating in friendly matches, and these teams included Killybegs Shamrocks, Tyrconnells, Carrick Swifts, Drimgorman Swifts and Ballintra Hibernians. It is evident that association football was still gaining popularity in the south of the county around this time, and the league committee decided that a divisional system would be more appropriate. At a meeting held in Boyle's Hotel, Ramelton, on 9 February 1898, the draw was made for the cup, with Convoy Celtic paired with Ramelton, Buncrana scheduled to meet Castlefin Rangers, and Ardara Emeralds drawn against Convoy Mills. Donegal Celtic received a home draw against Raphoe and the final was fixed for 26 March.[107] The league had been divided into three divisions. Division one consisted of two southern teams: Donegal Celtic and Ardara Emeralds. Division two was made up clubs from east Donegal: Raphoe, Castlefin Rangers, Convoy Mills and Convoy Celtic. Division three consisted of two northern-based teams: Buncrana and Ramelton. There were no teams from the west affiliated with the association for this season, and there is no evidence as to why cup specialists Derrybeg declined to take part. Similarly, of the original 1894/5 cup entrants, Cranford, Cratlagh, Letterkenny, Kerrykeel, Swilly Rangers and Milford Swifts had all disappeared from the competition.

THE END OF THE COUNTY DONEGAL FOOTBALL ASSOCIATION

Donegal Celtic progressed to play eastern winners Raphoe in a match that was scheduled for 28 February.[108] Buncrana beat Ramelton 2-0 to top their group and qualify for the play-offs.[109] Despite Donegal Celtic defeating Raphoe, they were later removed from the competition when Raphoe protested that they had fielded Charles Donnell, a Strabane Heroes player who had played in the North-west Junior Cup. Raphoe and Buncrana were then scheduled to play in the Shield Final on Easter Monday, 11 April 1898, in Rathmullan, after which the association's AGM was to be held.[110] However, there are no reports on this meeting in the issues of the *Derry Journal* which followed, although it is evident that Buncrana were easy winners of the shield by nine goals to two.[111] This was the last report of the season recorded in the newspaper, and the County Donegal FA folded after this. The winners of the cup were not acknowledged at the time, although it was noted in 1909 that Ramelton defeated Buncrana in the Cup Final.[112] It is apparent that the problems already identified were simply too great for the organising committee to cope with and the withdrawal of the majority of their initial clubs and some of their significant officers did little to help the association's growth. By the beginning of March 1898, the cup had still not been returned to the organising committee.[113]

ASSOCIATION FOOTBALL IN BALLYSHANNON

While it is difficult to establish the amount of interaction between army barracks and local soccer clubs in Donegal, the revival of association football in Ballyshannon in the south of the county in 1896 appears to be due to the Dorset Regiment, who were stationed at the local Rock Barracks at the time. Neal Garnham has also claimed that military involvement was significant to soccer's development and 'in setting standards of play', despite some disapproval from locals.[114] In 1882, there had been attempts to get soccer up and running in the town but this appears to have been an unsuccessful venture. A fifteen-a-side soccer match had been played between Bundoran and Ballyshannon selections in the spring of 1889, with both sides struggling with the art of taking a throw-in, and continuously finding touch with their attempts to pass.[115] Relations between the sides soured when Ballyshannon refused to continue their ties with their seaside-resort rivals, one excuse being given that the club had decided 'to neither practice, nor play any matches during Lent', which suggests that they would have had a strong Roman Catholic administration.[116]

Cricket was played in Ballyshannon throughout that summer, with the local members of the legal profession instrumental in arranging this, and attempts to reorganise the soccer club in November ended with those present at the meeting signalling their intention to form a rugby club, of which little appears to have been recorded.[117] The Ballyshannon-based *Donegal Vindicator* carried a report on cockfighting in April 1891, in which it claimed 'over 300 boys, youths and men assembled not far from the town to witness this bestial sport'.[118] This activity had been condemned at the late Mass the previous Sunday by the Revd P. Kelly, and the newspaper expressed hopes that those involved would find 'some innocent pastime that would work off their bottled up energies'.[119] This was their only day off work, and, while football and camán were encouraged, the writer felt that 'if the manly sport be too sternly suppressed on the plea of desecrating the Sunday assuredly young men will find some other way of amusing themselves'.[120] Lawn tennis and cricket continued in the town for the wealthier classes, and any attempts to form a soccer club in the next few years received little interest. While it is hard to ascertain precisely when the military took up their post at the Rock Barracks, they would prove to have a strong impact on the locals' sporting interest and help bring about the development of association football in Ballyshannon in the second half of the 1890s.

THE 2ND DORSET REGIMENT

In February 1897, the *Donegal Vindicator* noted that the association game had been in decline in the town in 1896, and was clear about who had helped re-establish it: '[when] the military commenced to practice, the Ballyshannon men took up courage, with the result that a new club was organised under the title of the Erne Football Club'.[121] It was to the nearby Rock Barracks that Erne FC looked for a challenge match after their foundation on 25 February 1896. This proposal lead to a detachment of the 2nd Dorset Regiment becoming heavily involved in the Ballyshannon community's sporting activities until they left for Derry in September of that year.[122] The Erne club's initial meeting, held in the Carrickboy Male NS, was well attended and a challenge was sent to the soldiers. John McAdam, proprietor of the *Donegal Vindicator*, became president, while fishing-tackle maker James Rogan (captain), E. McNulty (treasurer), and national school teacher Denis Nyhan (secretary), a Cork native, all took on their respective posts within the club.[123] On Wednesday 11 March, the club played its first match, 'before a large assemblage of spectators', in a field lent by farmer John Cummins.[124] The *Donegal Independent* vividly described the event:

> A stranger coming in from Belleek on that day would believe he was very near the famous Derby race course, as the bright shining jerseys of the civilians, under their capt. Mr Rogan, marched onto the field and looked splendid. We believe they were specially ordered from the new Hosiery establishment started by the Sisters of Mercy … the soldiers were dressed differently, having come to the field with short trousers and shins bare. The ground being in a bad slippery condition it was a wonder none of them got hurt. The soldiers were by far the lighter team.[125]

Despite their lack of team shirts, the Dorsets apparently came out on top by 4-3. They 'played a nice fast passing game' and were 'much superior to the home team in their dribbling tactics'.[126] However, the *Donegal Vindicator* was less than enthusiastic about the event in their report of the game, which they claimed ended in a draw. They illustrated some of the problems that dogged local soccer at the time, 'The rules were not well understood by either side … fouls were quite unknown and free-kicks not frequent. The referee was, as usual, well abused by the spectators and he seemed to deserve it.'[127] A week later the 'Young Bloods', a team composed of the local youths was formed and it was claimed that 'football has taken a firm hold on Ballyshannon at the present time'.[128] In April, the *Donegal Vindicator* highlighted this upsurge in soccer activity in the area:

> Football is buck jumping among all classes of upper and lower down society in Ballyshannon at present. It is football in the morning, at mid-day and even over the punch at night, nothing but football. It would be risky to say how many clubs have sprung into existence since the 'Erne' was formed a few weeks ago, but there must be at least a half a dozen.[129]

The practical and somewhat prophetic reporter advised these local clubs that they should stick together and combine into one if they were to challenge any of the bigger teams in Ulster. They were also advised to get an enclosed pitch with a stand and start collecting gates if they wanted to survive.[130]

The Dorsets played a number of friendlies against local teams and were soon the team to beat. It appears the 'sogers' were unbeaten in these matches and relied heavily on their impressive goalkeeper Tarpin (who, it was reported, was worth five players) and the unknown white-shirted forward with the hard, accurate shot.[131] After playing the local Belleek team, the sides were entertained in Mr Cleary's under the care of Corporal Willis.[132] While the Dorsets refused to play a representative Ballyshannon team, it is clear that their team was well liked by the local clubs and the community, and the *Donegal Vindicator* claimed, 'the town owes a debt of gratitude for the sport they have given the game. It will be news to the soldiers to learn that there has not been a football kicked in the town for five years.'[133]

Above left: John McAdam, first president of Erne FC and proprietor of the *Donegal Vindicator.* (Courtesy of John Ward)

Above right: James Sproule Myles, founder of Ballyshannon Swifts FC. (Courtesy of the National Library of Ireland)

The Ballyshannon based detachment of the regiment showed their appreciation to the local Workhouse committee, who had lent them their field for football, by giving a concert for the inmates in the Rock Hall on Thursday 7 May. It was later claimed, 'that they have been eminently successful is undeniable, and the large and fashionable gathering which filled the Rock Hall was testimony to the popularity of the Dorsets. The military band from Enniskillen was an additional attraction and helped to fill the house.'[134] The regiment also fielded cricket teams and took part in the Ballyshannon Show tug of war competition in August.[135] Although four of their soldiers were attacked in a Bundoran public house, which led to a court case in September, it was stated that, 'the Dorsets have on the whole been very popular among the town's [Ballyshannon's] people – especially the officers and non-coms'.[136] The last detachment left on the train for Derry on Thursday 17 September at 2.45p.m. and it appears that they were replaced by the Engineers.[137]

Local matches went into decline for a short period, but by the beginning of 1897 things were up and running again. It soon became the norm for teams in the south Donegal area to organise local matches, with post-match refreshments and entertainment provided for the visitors in a local hotel and a return match fixed for the following week on fields lent by farmers or property owners.

SPROULE MYLES AND THE SWIFTS FOOTBALL CLUB

By March 1897, the Erne Football Club had a new local rival in the Swifts team, who were organised by merchant James Sproule Myles, later described as 'the life of sport in Ballyshannon'.[138] A Presbyterian, born in 1877, he was the son of John Myles of Milltown House, who had held the position of petty sessions clerk 'for over forty years', and as a merchant, was reported to be 'probably the most extensive in the North-west'.[139] According to John B. Cunningham, 'the Myles family were the last of the merchant shipping families of Ballyshannon' and had arrived in Ballyshannon in 1607 with the forces of Queen Elizabeth.[140]

Sproule Myles did not limit himself to association football, and by October 1898 he was organising rugby in the town, having had experience of this sport with City of Derry Rugby Club. Despite difficulties in finding fifteen men from the Ballyshannon area with sufficient knowledge of the sport and enough interest to take part, he did manage to organise a few friendly matches against Enniskillen around that time. In 1899, Myles, later acknowledged as 'a man of powerful physique and a noted athlete in his youth', was part of the Ireland rugby team which visited Canada, where he broke his leg.[141] Twice wounded in the Great War, he received the Military Cross for bravery and later served as an Independent TD in the Dáil.[142]

LADIES' INVOLVEMENT IN ASSOCIATION FOOTBALL IN DONEGAL

Soccer clubs from south and south-west Donegal continued to send reports of their friendly matches to the local press throughout 1898. Teams such as Meenareen Wanderers and Straleel Rovers from the parish of Kilcar were involved in these, and the playing of soccer in this south-west area will be specifically looked at in chapter four. It was also recorded that at Kilbarron Rangers' friendly with the Erne first XI in mid-March there were 'about 800 spectators present'.[143] North-Donegal-based teams continued to play against visiting ships' crews, and, on the same weekend, Swilly Rangers thrashed the footballers of the HMS *Jason* by 6-1, 'before a large crowd of spectators, the fairer sex being largely represented'.[144] In general, however, women's involvement in local sport received little acknowledgement in the Donegal press around this time, other than recognition of attendance at matches or help given to clubs' fundraising concerts.

THE VINDICATOR CUP, 1898

In November of that year the 'Vindicator Silver Challenge Cup' was organised in Ballyshannon and drew entries from Donegal Celtic, Ballintra Hibernians, Ballyshannon Swifts, Beleek Rose Isles and Ballyshannon Erne '98s. This was to be 'the first cup ever competed for in this district' and gold medals for the winners were to be supplied by local solicitor and president of the organisation, Michael Maguire, a brother of the Very Revd Dr Edward.[145] The *Donegal Independent* later recorded that the competition was known as 'The South Donegal Challenge Cup', a title that did not sit well with their rival newspaper, particularly as John McAdam was both the proprietor of the *Donegal Vindicator* and the chairman of the cup committee.[146] His newspaper described the trophy for the winners, 'It is solid silver, hall marked, nine inches high and beautifully engraved. The cup stands upon an ebonised pedestal and is as neat and valuable as anything of the kind in the north of Ireland.'[147]

The final between the Swifts and the Ernes was played on 26 December 1898 on the Swifts' ground in Ballyshannon, and, according to the *Donegal Independent*, approximately 2,000 spectators attended.[148] The *Donegal Vindicator* claimed there were spectators present from Killybegs, Sligo, Enniskillen and Omagh, and 'many ladies graced the enclosure with their presence'.[149] This match had a bit of additional spice, as the Ernes team were fielding some former Swifts players. A disallowed goal and an injury to Sproule Myles proved costly for the Swifts, as the Ernes held on for a 2–1 win, but this result was met with a protest, the type of which had become commonplace in competitive Donegal soccer.

At the end of January the issue had still not been resolved, despite witnesses being called to a meeting and the referee, A.C. Crawford, CE, giving his account to the committee. The Swifts team protested on six points: that their disallowed goal was legitimate; that Ernes had used threatening and abusive language on the pitch; that their team had been subjected to off-the-ball attacks; that the referee hadn't played enough time and that he had failed to take into account the time wasted by the eventual winners during the second half, and that spectators had interfered with the running of the match. A vote was taken by ballot and a replay was decided upon.[150] This did not satisfy Mr Crawford, however. He was determined to prove that he was correct and that the result on the field could not be reversed. He took the trouble of writing to the editor of the London-based *Athletic Record*, who replied, agreeing that the referee's decisions and result was final.[151] This was further confirmed by John Reid, the secretary of the IFA in Belfast.[152] This was the last Vindicator Cup competition to be played, as, despite calls in the local press for another try during the next few years, there was not enough interest taken to organise further competitions. In November 1901, there were only two entries (this was obviously insufficient) and friendly matches became the order of the day in Ballyshannon again until 1905.[153]

RENEWED INTEREST IN GAELIC GAMES

Not everyone was happy to see sports such as association football, rugby, tennis, hockey and billiards take centre stage in the Ballyshannon area. Any mention of Gaelic games in the Ballyshannon press was rare at this time. In May 1897, 'An Interested Gael', writing from Rathmore (Ballyshannon) to the editor of the *Donegal Vindicator*, expressed hopes that Gaelic football and hurling would be implemented in the county. He listed Donegal as being amongst eleven counties that had not introduced these sports up to that point. He also wished to see Donegal represented at the Ulster Convention, and for hurling, 'the grand old game of our forefathers', to begin in Donegal and in Ulster.[154] There were no replies to this letter in the paper, but it is interesting to note that a Gaelic League committee was formed in Ballyshannon at the beginning of January 1898.[155] (This organisation will be addressed in the next chapter.) By the end of November 1898 there were calls in the local press from 'A lover of the Gaelic', residing in Mountcharles, for those in the south Donegal parish of Inver to begin Gaelic classes and become more heavily involved in the Gaelic movement which was sweeping the country.[156] The parishioners of Inver would feature prominently in the setting up of the Gaelic Athletic Association in Mountcharles in 1905, but up until then soccer dominated the sporting headlines from the county. The lack of GAA activity in Donegal at the turn of the century was highlighted in an article written by Patrick Dougherty from Carrigart in the north-west of the county and first published in *The Irish Homestead* in February 1902:

> Even once popular sports, such as handball, hurling and the other old fashioned games, so dear to the lad of twenty years ago, are almost 'dead as a door nail' and if you said 'camán' to a little lad now, he would think you were talking Greek, and run to the school master, to find out what it meant.[157]

DONEGAL CELTIC AND THE TYRONE AND DONEGAL FOOTBALL CUP, 1903

In terms of geographical difficulties, it is also clear that some eastern and northern association football teams found it easier to affiliate with the Derry and Tyrone soccer leagues at the beginning of the 1900s. Lifford and Buncrana were perhaps most notable for this, as organisation of transport to matches had to be practical. Donegal Celtic were able to avail of the train line in order to participate in and win the Tyrone and Donegal Football Cup in May 1903. In the decisive match they defeated Newtownstewart Rangers at the Recreation Park, Strabane, on 29 May, having drawn with their Tyrone rivals on three previous occasions.[158] This victory was well received in Donegal Town:

> There were great rejoicings in Donegal on hearing the result of the match. The Young Bloods' Fife and Drum Band met the players at the railway station and paraded the town in honour of the victory. A number of tar barrels were lighted

> in the Diamond on the arrival of the team, and cheers heartily responded to. By courtesy of the Donegal Gaelic League the Market House was procured and a dance was held, in which the members of the team and their supporters and friends enjoyed themselves until daybreak on Saturday morning.[159]

It is worth noting that the Gaelic League in the town had no problem accommodating the local soccer club at this point. It is also significant that the following February, the Donegal Celtic club held a successful concert which consisted of Irish dancing and singing in the Temperance Hall.[160] By November 1904, Buncrana, Convoy, Castlefin and Donegal Celtic were all participating in the North-west of Ireland Football Association Junior Cup and the remainder of the teams in the county had to make do with friendly matches.[161] But 1905 would see a change in sporting affairs. The Gaelic Athletic Association would provide stiff competition for soccer as the Gaelic Revival began to take effect throughout the county, with nationalists such as Seumas MacManus seeing it as their duty to eradicate British culture from their native land.

CONCLUSION

It is evident that those running soccer in Derry City were highly influential, both directly and indirectly, in helping the game spread to the north-east of Donegal. The crews of ships docked around Lough Swilly also contributed to the level of interest in the game around this area, by challenging local teams to occasional matches. The notion of Muscular Christianity was fundamental to the organisation of association football clubs in County Donegal, where local businessmen and those with influence in society saw it as their duty to provide a more positive pastime for the youth of their villages; in some cases, clubs came into existence from other organisations which had already been in place. While the North-west FA initially provided some competitive stability for a number of clubs in the north-east Donegal area, Daniel Deeney's frustration at these clubs' inability to match the Derry clubs' standard of play led to the setting up of the first Donegal soccer body in 1894.

However, while the new organisation was met initially with enthusiasm, the league and cup competitions did not receive much public support and matches were poorly advertised in the local press. The transport network meant that clubs from other areas outside the north-east, with the exception of Derrybeg Celtic, were slow to join up. Internal disputes and the failure by a number of prominent clubs to acknowledge the rules laid down by the association meant that it could not develop in a successful manner. The physical barrier of the Blue Stack Mountains also meant that those in the south of the county were somewhat isolated from this heart of soccer activity. Financially, the organisation struggled and failed to install a proper method of collecting admission fees at matches, an issue which Metcalfe has identified as being the determining factor in whether a soccer club would flourish or deteriorate.[162]

In the south of the county there was a strong military influence in the organisation of association football, with a detachment of the Dorset Regiment raising the profile of the game in Ballyshannon. However, competitive soccer in this area was also not without administrative difficulties. The growth of the Donegal Celtic club was highlighted in their victory over their Tyrone rivals and this success was positively acknowledged by the local Gaelic League at the time. The train line also meant that, by the beginning of the 1900s, they could travel north to compete.

Overall, the county was still handicapped by the lack of industry and a widespread method of transport, often crucial factors in the growth of sport in a region. It must be noted, however, that the 1890s did see the establishment of quite a number of soccer clubs throughout Donegal and at that time the geographical parameters where soccer would flourish, particularly in the north-east region, were beginning to be laid down.

3

THE EVANS CUP AND THE DONEGAL GAA COUNTY BOARD

'It is a great pity that while the other counties of Ireland have awakened to the fact that they are Irish … Donegal alone, one of the most Gaelic counties in Ireland, should not realise its duty.'

Seumas MacManus[1]

ASSOCIATION FOOTBALL IN DONEGAL IN 1905

At the beginning of 1905 there were a number of notices in the local press illustrating a desire for a return to competitive soccer. On 20 January, a gentleman describing himself as 'footballer', while acknowledging the difficulties involved in travelling, suggested a cup competition be run with the organisation's headquarters based in Letterkenny. He felt that a cup-tie structure run on a divisional basis would be a success, as 'with a referee backed up by the association this murmuring against his decisions that characterizes country football would cease'.[2] His optimism was not strong enough to convince anyone to reply, but in the south-west of the county one man had both the interest and the means to take action.

Robert E.L. Evans was the youngest son of miller John Evans and Elizabeth Smith, and their family had resided at the Mill in Ardara by the Owentocker River until they were evicted from their home in the 1885, apparently for failing to pay the rent.[3]

Evans's Mill. (Courtesy of Dympna Duff)

THE EVANS CUP

By 1905, Mr Evans was living on Willows Road, Birmingham, but clearly he was still a popular figure in the Ardara area. In January of that year it was claimed in the *Derry Journal* that 'his genial, affable and unaffected manners, although possessing unlimited means, make him a general favourite, and his advent to Ardara is looked forward to by those who know his family connections with much interest'.[4] In the same article on 'The Evans Silver Cup', the arrangements which had been made to organise a soccer cup competition in the Ardara area were published, along with plans to establish the cup committee of which Robert E.L. Evans was to be honorary president.[5] This was a cup donated by Mr Evans, who, while he was back on holiday, had been inspired to purchase the trophy by the sight of a group of Ardara boys playing soccer.

The goblet-shaped cup was made of solid silver and was gold lined. It stood on an oak pedestal and measured around fifteen inches in height. On one side, the cup was inscribed with a harp, underneath which were the words, 'in sports, as in things national, success, if obtained honestly, merits esteem, but, if dishonourably, deserves contempt'. The trophy was also inscribed on the other side as 'The South Donegal Football Challenge Cup' and was to be given permanently to the team that won it three years in a row. Those present at the initial meeting on Thursday 26 January 1905, in the local reading rooms, included the Revd Daniel Stephens, who took the chair. Revd Stephens, a Ballyshannon man, had been arrested along with Fr McFadden during the Land War in Falcarragh and had later survived an attempt on his life.[6] Others who were involved in the organisation of the competition included: William J. McGinley, District Inspector of the RIC; Peter O'Clery, Inland Revenue Officer; Michael McNelis, Clerk of the Glenties Union; national school teachers Thomas Gavigan and P.J. Bradden; Mr Lee of the RIC; carpenter and cooper Henry Cannon; post office official Peter McCaul; student John Cassidy; draper Patrick Gildea; Joseph (farmer) and James (shop assistant) McHugh, and John Sharpe, spirit and grocery merchant. A committee was to be formed at a later date, as Dr Charles Falvey, Wood House, was absent from the meeting.[7] Revd Stephens, District Inspector W.J. McGinley and Thomas Gavigan were present at Dr Falvey's wedding on Easter Monday 1905, and Peter O'Clery had acted as his best man.[8]

Wedding of Dr Charles Falvey and Margaret Fallon, 1905. (Courtesy of Malachi McCloskey)

LOCAL CONNECTIONS

It is also worth noting that Henry Cannon was a friend of Robert Evans and, along with his brother James, would act as a 'gilly' during Evans's fishing trips on the nearby river Owenea.[9] These brothers featured prominently in the Ardara Emeralds Football Club, both as players and administrators. Twenty-nine-year-old Michael McNelis of the Nesbitt Arms Hotel had been secretary of the Ardara Agricultural and Industrial Show and had been appointed secretary of the local golf club in 1899.[10] A number of these men were also prominent in organising the local agricultural show, and in August 1902, O'Clery, Dr Falvey, McNelis, Gavigan, Bradden and Sharpe all contributed to the organisation of the Ardara Gaelic League Feis.[11] The soccer competition was to be an annual one and the cup took pride of place in the window of Brennan's hotel on the main street in Ardara.

NAME	ADDRESS	AGE	OCCUPATION
Robert E.L. Evans	Willows Park, Birmingham	Unknown	Miller's son
Charles H. Falvey	Woodhouse	25	Medical Doctor
William Joseph McGinley	Unknown	Unknown	DI, RIC
Daniel Stephens	Parochial House	31	Revd, Catholic Church
Henry Cannon	The Diamond	29	Carpenter & Boat Builder
Peter O'Clery	Unknown	39	Inland Revenue Officer
Thomas Gavigan	Cranaghboy	37	NS Teacher
Patrick J. Bradden	Doohill	39	NS Teacher
John Cassidy	The Diamond	18	Student
Thomas Dorrian	West End	27	Farmer
Peter Molloy	Main Street	35	Merchant
John Boyle	Main Street	24	Flesher
Joseph McHugh	West End	28	Farmer
James McHugh	West End	34	Asst. Shopkeeper
Patrick Gildea	Main Street	30	Draper
Michael McNelis	Main Street	29	Clerk of Glenties Union
John Sharpe	Main Street	34	Spirit Merchant/Grocer
Peter McCaul	The Diamond	20	Post Office Asst.

Table 1: The 1905 Evans Cup Organising Committee.

Ardara Emeralds FC *c.*1900. (Courtesy of John McConnell)

Clearly, the majority of these men were based in the town area (Evans being one of the exceptions, with teachers Bradden and Gavigan living a few miles out of town) and many would have been seen as pillars of society. All were relatively young, with free time and some money in their pockets; most appear to have been single. Many had previous experience of administrative work and some had been members of other local committees involved in creating an identity, entertainment, and a voice for their area. Significantly, it could also be said that they were interested in socialising together. Mike Huggins has identified 'the arrival in the town of an enthusiastic individual who could gather round him a group of keen friends'[12] as one of the keys in the diffusion of soccer in north-east England between 1876 and 1890, and in the case of association football in Ardara, Evans seems to fit this mould in initially helping to organise a cup competition for the locality.

As previously mentioned, the Ardara Emeralds Football Club had been founded in 1891 after a group of local young men organised a concert to raise funds to form an athletic club in the town for the benefit of the local youths.[13] It appears they decided on an association football club, as the Ardara Emeralds FC were holding fortnightly meetings by the autumn of that year, and could claim that, 'since the club has been started the merchants and people of Ardara have given it their warmest support'.[14] They also felt that they could rely on the support of the clergy and that, 'our local gentry and sportspeople are deeply interested in the welfare of the youth of the district'.[15]

C.M. Brennan was the club's first captain, while H. McLoone was appointed secretary.[16] However, there was little recorded in the local press about their development other than a local match against Narin FC the following month, and their concert and ball which was held in January 1892 with the help of Dr John E.Langan, who again gave his store for the occasion.[17] Little is known about the club until their appearance in the aforementioned County Donegal Challenge Cup in 1897/8 and these appearances seem to be their only competitive matches in that decade.

SEUMAS MACMANUS AND THE GAELIC LEAGUE

Robert Evans's enthusiasm was not shared by Seumas MacManus, described by a contemporary as 'practically the founder of the Gaelic movement in Mountcharles and district'[18] and the leading activist in the Gaelic Revival in Donegal. In 1905, he expressed his contempt in the *Derry Journal* for the playing of what he clearly saw as a 'foreign' sport.

Born on New Year's Eve 1868 and educated at the Model School in Enniskillen, MacManus had left his job as Principal in Glencoagh NS in 1897 to concentrate on his writing career and the promotion of nationalism.[19] However it would also appear that he was forced to resign his post in October 1897 after the education board 'raised some questions regarding his name being connected with the '98 centenary celebrations'.[20]

The Gaelic League, founded in July 1893 by Douglas Hyde and Eoin MacNeill, 'aspired to be a non-sectarian and non-political organisation, which would provide an inclusivist forum for those committed to the language'.[21] According to Helen Meehan, Seumas MacManus was one of those responsible for founding the Gaelic League in Donegal and had been secretary of the branch in Donegal Town.[22] By 1895, the Gaelic League in Donegal was holding meetings in places where 'some type of Gaelic society was already in existence' and MacManus addressed the crowd at the first meeting, which was held in Brockagh near Glenfin in the east of the county.[23] Tom Hunt has established that Gaelic League branches were involved in the founding of GAA clubs in Longford, Westmeath, Dublin, Derry and Fermanagh at the beginning of the twentieth century[24] and there is also evidence to suggest that a number of west Tyrone GAA clubs, founded prior to 1900, had their origins in the movement.[25] David Hassan also believes that the League 'assisted the promotion of Gaelic games through their inclusion in the *Feiseanna* or festival programmes'.[26]

There is evidence to suggest that there was strong Gaelic League involvement in the camán clubs of Ballyshannon and Bundoran in 1904. A hurling club had been formed at a meeting of the Bundoran Gaelic League in April 1904, held under the presidency of Revd J. Merron.[27] At the Ballyshannon hurling club céilidh held in May of that year, it was recorded that the Rock Hall was 'well filled, principally with members of the Ballyshannon, Bundoran and Belleek [Fermanagh] branches of the Gaelic League'.[28] However, these GAA clubs were temporarily in decline the following year, without sufficient support, and it appears that the Ballyshannon club's deterioration was due to the inactivity of that town's Gaelic League.[29] Decline and re-establishment of Gaelic League branches was a common occurrence at this time.[30]

Although it is difficult to establish exactly how many Gaelic League clubs were operating in Donegal by 1905, there is evidence to suggest that members of its branches in south Donegal were involved in GAA clubs after the foundation of the county board and were instrumental in organising Gaelic football and hurling through their social events. Certainly there were Gaelic League branches in Mountcharles, Donegal Town, Bundoran and Ballyshannon by 1905 although precisely how many members became involved in GAA clubs in Donegal is unknown.

SEUMAS MACMANUS'S PRESS CAMPAIGN BEGINS

In a letter to the editor, published in the *Derry Journal* edition dated 1 March 1905, Mr MacManus asserted that:

> … it is a great pity that while the other counties of Ireland have awakened to the fact that they are Irish, and have adopted again their own Irish games in preference to games introduced by the foreigner, Donegal alone, one of the most Gaelic counties in Ireland, should not realise its duty.[31]

He also claimed that the majority of football clubs in his native county were engaged in the playing of association football and requested for this to come to an end when the season finished. Indeed, the previous month an Inishowen gentleman had appealed in the local press for someone to sponsor a soccer cup for their area as there were teams in Malin, Clonmany, Culdaff, Moville and Carndonagh without cup competition.[32]

MacManus called for a meeting to take place to organise a more widespread playing of Gaelic games within Donegal, but his tirade did not end there. His emotional appeal illustrated his patriotism and he concluded, rather

Seumas MacManus. (Courtesy of the County Donegal Archives)

fanatically, by requesting that the Evans Cup be given up for the sport of Gaelic football. He felt that this would help strengthen the revival of the Irish game: it was clear that MacManus was determined to establish Gaelic games as the number-one pastime in the county. This was the start of a nationalist campaign in south Donegal to prevent the playing of association football in the area and encourage the spread of Gaelic games. He was clearly influenced by 'the Ban', which had been reinstated by the GAA at the beginning of February 1905. The new ban stated that 'persons who play rugby, soccer, hockey, cricket or any imported games shall be suspended for two years of playing such games'.[33] While there has been much controversy over this issue in Irish society throughout the twentieth century, Mike Cronin believes that it was introduced 'to ensure the popularity and success of the Association, and in response to the political spirit which dominated Irish life at the time'.[34]

SUPPORT FOR THE EVANS CUP

While there is no specific reference to the Ban in the *Derry Journal* at this time, or indeed any mention of any vigilante committees, it is clear that this type of sentiment against the playing of 'foreign games' could certainly be found in the south of the county. However, it is evident that not everybody in Donegal was in favour of the ideology of the ban in 1905. In a letter to the editor of the *Derry Journal* written on 18 April and signed 'Commonsense', the writer complained about MacManus's interpretation of soccer being played under English rules, and concluded by stating that 'the Ardara cup committee had no justification for following MacManus's appeal to donate the Evans Cup to Gaelic football'.[35]

The Evans Cup committee did not, however, manage to organise any fixtures until the following autumn. The *Derry Journal* of 15 September 1905 reported that, before 'a splendid assembly of members', chairman Henry Cannon expressed regret on behalf of the committee that the competition had not taken place.[36] This was the first meeting of the new season, but the matter which had so much aggrieved Seumas MacManus was not decided upon until the beginning of November. At the weekly debate held in the town in which Revd Stephens organised reading for young members of local clubs, 'the debate – "Which should be played, Gaelic or Association football?" – was argued ably' and 'it was resolved by an overwhelming majority' to continue the competition under soccer rules.[37]

Although, as events turned out in the future, many members of the Ardara club would find themselves involved in Gaelic games, it is worth noting that at this point they refused to give in to the pressure from MacManus to succumb to patriotic feelings and emotional blackmail, and, having drawn up and printed their rules, they went ahead with their soccer competition in February 1906. The political and social climate of the time can be illustrated in the fact that only three teams – Ardara Emeralds, Killybegs Emeralds and Donegal United – entered the tournament.[38]

Killybegs Emeralds had been founded in the Hibernian Hall, Bridge Street on 15 August 1896 'by the parish priest at the time, Fr John Sweeney, and other local businessmen', not unlike their Ardara counterparts, 'for the benefit of the youth of the town and parish'.[39] A number of these businessmen had been involved in the local regatta committee and wanted to include field games such as soccer in the events.[40] According to Moira Mallon, soccer had been brought to the town in the early 1890s by engineers and workmen from the city of Derry who were working on the railway into Killybegs, which opened in 1893.[41] In 1896, St Columba's Marine Industrial School was set up and Scottish boatwrights would teach the schoolboys soccer in their spare time.[42] Derry workmen building the new McGinley residence were also instrumental in strengthening the soccer club, and these early developments paved the way for the strong interest in soccer in the town, which continues to the present day, with the St Catherine's Football Club.[43]

Above left: The Revd Daniel Stephens. (Courtesy of the National Library of Ireland)

Above right: Killybegs Emeralds, 1904. (Courtesy of Moira Mallon)

CUMANN NA NGAEDHEAL

Cumann na nGaedheal had been formed in 1900 'as a focus for a wide variety of literary and other cultural groupings', with Arthur Griffith its founder.[44] Diarmaid Ferriter believes that 'it soon became an IRB front' after its foundation.[45] It is clear that there was a strong nationalistic feeling running through the activities of the branches in the parish of Inver, which lies in the south of Donegal. The members of the Ethna Carberry Mountcharles branch of Cumann na nGaedheal were the primary advocates of the playing of Gaelic games in County Donegal throughout 1905. Founded in 1902, in their efforts to promote Irish culture the branch organised outings to nearby villages and towns where marches would precede camán matches, nationalist songs and speeches.[46] They put a strong emphasis on eradicating the playing of soccer from Irish society and this is illustrated in their reports in the *Derry Journal*.

At the beginning of April 1905, they set up what they believed to 'probably be the first camoguidheacht (camogie) club in the north-west' of Ireland, for their twenty lady members.[47] There were also thirty young men playing camán, and an overwhelming majority voted for Gaelic Athletic rules to be used in the playing of football, while an appeal was made to the Ardara soccer club to donate the Evans Cup.

INCREASED PRESSURE ON ASSOCIATION FOOTBALL CLUBS

A district council of the Gaelic League (or Coiste Ceanntair) met in Donegal Town on 8 April 1905. Amongst those in attendance included the vice-president, solicitor P.M. Gallagher, who took the chair, and Seumas MacManus. Resolutions were passed at this meeting to encourage the playing of Gaelic games and to 'discard the English Association football'.[48] Again, there was a request made to the Ardara committee to give up the Evans Cup, and those present also stressed the importance of buying Irish-manufactured goods.

Attempts were then made to get the local soccer club to switch to Gaelic football. Solicitor P.M. Gallagher also presided over a meeting of the Donegal United football club which took place on 16 April in their rooms, with around twenty people in attendance. There it was decided that they would stop playing soccer. It was declared that, 'the principle subject before the meeting was the restoration of Gaelic games in the town of the Four Masters –which town they rightly consider should show good example to the remainder of the county'.[49] They also appointed two delegates, John McBrearty and John McGinty, to attend a football conference in Ardara in the hope of promoting the national pastimes and 'the general adoption of the Gaelic games throughout south-west Donegal'.[50] Although there were later 'vigilante committees' organised in the county, during the 1930s, this appears to be the first mention of a number of delegates being organised to try and enforce a ban on the playing of association football in Donegal.

SUPPORT FROM THE CLERGY

In May 1905, the Ethna Carberry branch of Cumann na nGaedheal stepped up their patriotic activities. Seumas MacManus knew the value of having the clergy involved in local activities and a number of these were encouraged to support the development of Gaelic games in south Donegal. Nationalistic fervour was again high at the branch's excursion to Glenties on Sunday 4 June. Local curate Canon McFadden, who had moved from Gweedore, urged a revival of the Irish language and pastimes, and also encouraged doing away with foreign language, games and dances. Again, soccer bore the brunt in their encouragement of all things Irish – Canon McFadden claimed that, 'the time has come when Anglo-Saxon football should be crushed out' and he vehemently attacked 'the Anglo-Saxons of Ardara and Killybegs' whom he claimed, 'loved the foreign game as they do their king and if they must play the game of their country, England, they should be sent to play at the back of the Croach in Airgid, where no Irishmen would see them'.[51] Clearly he had changed his views on association football since his earlier involvement with Derrybeg Celtic.

Neal Garnham believes that at the beginning of the twentieth century, 'soccer was indeed simply seen as "foreign" in nature, and therefore inherently unsuitable for playing by Irishmen'. He also claims that the English game 'was seen by supporters of Gaelic games as an effeminate sport, unsuited to the manly Irish'. This was the type of view put forward by Archbishop Croke when, talking in general of foreign games, defined their players as 'degenerate dandies ... arrayed in light attire'.[52]

Camán matches were attracting large crowds of spectators from within the parish of Inver, and boys and girls were being encouraged to participate. It was claimed in the *Derry Journal* that at the Ethna Carberry branch outing to Croagh on 16 July, there were 700 'boys' in attendance. There was a large marching procession as the members sang 'March of the Camán Man'. After the goalless match between Inver and Croagh, there were nationalist speeches, songs and recitations, with local man Pádraig Mac Giolla Iosa leading renditions of 'Clann na nGaedeal go Deo'. The Mountcharles choir sang 'O'Donnell Abú' as spectators listened on the Knock rising above the playing field. Mac Giolla Iosa also delivered an address on 'the Duty of the Youth of Ireland' and plans were made for the Croagh boys to start a branch of the organisation. The entertainment concluded with a camán used in 1875 being wielded by the father of one of the players, and then presented to Mac Giolla Iosa for display at the Oireachtas Exhibition in Dublin.[53]

Three weeks later, at another local camán match, the Very Revd Dr Edward Maguire gave an address to a large crowd gathered on Inver Strand and he praised their efforts to revive the native games while 'killing off the games of the foreigner'.[54] It was agreed that two new teams, Killymard Celtic and Mountcharles Glen, were to be formed, and this illustrates the increasing popularity of camán in the area at this time and the growing nationalist spirit.

THE GRAND CAMÁN PARADE, 1905

Cumann na nGaedheal also organised céilís for their members, and at one of these, at the beginning of September 1905, in Croagh, situated near Dunkineely, chairman James Molloy again articulated the strong nationalistic theme running through the movement when he stated that he didn't want English songs or games played, or 'foreign' dances to be held in Donegal. He also stated that 'they had re-established their fine old game of camán' and congratulated the nearby Dunkineely club on organising camán and Gaelic football teams.[55]

At a meeting of the Derry GAA county board held that same month, Seumas MacManus was in attendance and encouraged the Derry members to speak Irish and to 'read the works of Mitchel, of Davis, and the other great men who had worked in trying times for Ireland'.[56] T. O'Flynn of the Derry board was convinced of the need to establish the GAA 'in the minds and hearts of the people', and saw 'the mutual co-operation of the clubs and the support of consistent nationalists' as being fundamental to this.[57] MacManus also felt that Derry would be a good centre for establishing Gaelic games in the north-west and hoped to see a number of Derry clubs at the Great Camán Parade, a demonstration to promote the Irish language and Gaelic games.[58] This was scheduled for Sunday 8 October in Mountcharles; arrangements were made and advertisements were placed in the *Derry Journal*.[59] MacManus was keen to promote the clean-living image of the Gael and encouraged those attending to stay sober that day. He also wanted to see a marching drill with camáns placed on shoulders.[60] General Manager of the Donegal lines, R.H. Livesay granted excursion trains from Derry, Ballyshannon and Killybegs and Charles O'Breslin of the Derry GAA County Committee met with representatives from a number of Derry clubs in the Magazine Rooms in the city on Tuesday 3 October to organise the trip, and to outline Seumas MacManus's timetable of events.[61]

Among the 2,000 people who attended the parade were captains of the local patriotically named camán teams, along with their Strabane and Clady counterparts. After Mass the procession marched to the strand, where the Very Revd Dr Edward Maguire took the chair. A letter of support from Bishop Patrick O'Donnell was read, in which he claimed that 'Irish games in Irish terms are the games for Irish people … no sports are so good for our people as those of native growth.'[62] He echoed the contemporary view of hurling and advised the youth of the country to take it up, 'Besides Irish football, a more manly game than camán for all classes of Irishmen it would be difficult to find; and surely it would be well if all our young people, men and women, had learned drill as children at school.'[63] Bishop O'Donnell also advocated swimming in the area, for practical reasons, and was keen to see an emphasis on temperance and fair play in sport. He concluded by stating that 'it is most gratifying to hear that our young athletes are fully conscious that stimulants are the very worst preparation for success in the games'.[64]

Above left: Canon McFadden. (Courtesy of the National Library of Ireland)

Above right: The Very Revd Dr Edward Maguire. (Courtesy of the National Library of Ireland)

After a number of speeches, a competition for the camán clubs took place. There were nine camán clubs from Derry and Tyrone in attendance and a competition was held between the newly formed clubs of the area and their Derry and Tyrone counterparts. A number of these Donegal clubs can be identified as having their origins in local branches of Cumann na nGaedheal, including: the Ethna Carberry team, Croagh; the Naomh Conaill team, Kilraine; the Thomas Davis club, Dunkineely, and the Lámh Dearg club, Mountcharles.[65] They were joined by other local camán clubs, such as: Ardaghey Old Celts; the Colmcille club, Lettermore; the John Mitchells club, Doorin; the Clann Conaill club, Brackey; the Four Masters club, Townawilly, and the True Gaels club of Meenabradan.[66] This patriotic naming of clubs after local or national figures was also common in Westmeath in the early twentieth century, where Hunt believes that it illustrated the growth of nationalism and the politicisation of Gaelic football and hurling clubs.[67] That day's sporting activity ended with Derry hurlers drawing with Tyrone in difficult conditions.[68]

THE FOUNDATION OF THE GAA COUNTY BOARD

This strong emphasis on Irish culture finally culminated in the forming of the Donegal GAA county board on Monday 23 October at a meeting organised by Seumas MacManus and the Ethna Carberry Cumann na nGaedheal branch. Held in MacIntyre's hotel in Mountcharles, the meeting was presided over by the Very Revd Dr Maguire and representatives were present from local areas such as Mountcharles, Doorin, Lettermore, Croagh and Ardaghey, and from neighbouring districts such as Kilraine, Ballintra and Laghey, who had made their way on horseback, on pushbike and on foot.[69] Teams were to be given three weeks to affiliate before the league fixtures would be drawn up. A trophy was to be purchased for the Aonach Camán winners and a cup was to be sought for the Gaelic football competition. The Camán final would be played in July 1906 at the Aonach an Dúin festival, which was being organised by Bishop O'Donnell, who was patron of the newly formed board. It was hoped that this fair would raise funds for the building of St Eunan's College in Letterkenny and that it would promote Irish industry and culture. The county was to be divided into two divisions, east and west, with national school teacher Alec McDyer of Kilraine, Glenties, in charge of the western area and John Dowds of Castlehill, Burt, a truant officer with the Education Board, acting as eastern secretary. The regions were divided as follows, 'West Donegal division to extend from the Drowes river, west of Bundoran, to Glen head, and from Pettigo to Fintown to Doochary (all of those places included). Ballybofey and Stranorlar, as well as the Rosses, consequently belonged to east Donegal for Gaelic Athletic purposes.'[70]

PRESS APPEAL

Donegal was to be represented in the Central Council of the GAA by the Very Revd Dr Edward Maguire, who was appointed west division delegate,[71] while Revd P. O'Doherty of Gweedore became eastern representative to the national body.[72] Provincially, the Very Revd Dr Maguire and P.A. Mooney were elected as members of the Ulster Council for the west division[73] and C. Ward of Letterkenny and John Dowds of Burt were chosen to represent the other side of the county.[74] Seumas MacManus's GAA rules and terms in Irish were published in the local press after the initial county board meeting, and he also suggested that 'the surest method of memorising is that of

Bishop Patrick O'Donnell.
(Courtesy of Canon Laverty)

taking the list in one's pocket (pasted on stiff paper or card-board) to *páirc na h-imearca* (the field of play) and consulting it as occasion arises'.[75] It was also hoped that the youth of the county would support the movement. The Very Revd Dr Maguire, Alec McDyer and John Dowds issued their manifesto 'to the patriotic young men of Donegal' in the *Derry Journal* published on Wednesday 15 November. They claimed that, while 'we have, to our shame, been West-British in many things', they had, in actual fact, been contributing to this state by 'making slaves of ourselves'. Now the time had come to leave this all behind and an appeal was made:

> ... to the youth of the county in general, and in particular to leading men (both young and old), in each district in the county where a Gaelic athletic club is not already formed, to found such at once, so that no district in Donegal may any longer lie under the reproach of lagging in shame when Ireland has arisen up and is casting from her the tokens of littleness and slavery.[76]

THE BALLDEARGS

Other nationalist organisations were keen to support the Gaelic games movement. At a meeting of the Donegal branch of the Ancient Order of Hibernians, which had taken place in the last week of October at the Shamrock Hall in Donegal Town, Brother Henry McCaffrey proposed to support the Gaelic League and to 'endeavour by every means in our power to organise a Gaelic football and hurling team'.[77] On Friday 20 October, he was elected treasurer at the founding of the Donegal Town Balldearg hurling and Gaelic football club at a meeting held in a factory lent by P.M. Gallagher, who was appointed chairman. Gallagher then gave an explanation of the rules of hurling and promised the use of his factory for the club's meetings, and agreed to distribute hurleys and a ball.[78] According to local historian Eamonn Monaghan, the Balldeargs 'owed their name to the red birthmark peculiar to the O'Donnell clan'.[79] As previously mentioned, membership of the Gaelic League and the GAA were closely linked in those day, and this seems to have been the case, with a number of members of this club having dual membership.[80] A Gaelic League branch was re-established in Donegal Town around this time and there is evidence to suggest that the GAA club was started in conjunction with this.[81]

THE CONTINUATION OF ASSOCIATION FOOTBALL IN DONEGAL TOWN

This is not to say that association football ground to a halt in Donegal Town. In a preview of the coming 'football season' in the town, it was claimed that 'a considerable number of the Association players have joined the Gaelic club with the result that the old club has been weakened'.[82] While the writer hoped that the two sporting bodies would co-operate, Donegal Celtic appointed the two former Donegal United delegates who had been sent to Ardara earlier in the year, John McGinty and John McBrearty, as captain and vice-captain respectively at their AGM at the beginning of October.[83]

Unfortunately there is no record of in the local press of those who lined out for the Balldearg Gaelic football in 1906 when the league began. The Balldearg camán team around this time was made up of a number of local tradesmen and farm workers and was run by Richard C. Bonner, who acted as player, trainer and referee and was later identified as being a member of the Gaelic League and Sinn Féin.[84] There is little evidence that any of these were involved in the Donegal Celtic team in 1906, but ironically the club would later be criticised for players' involvement in soccer matches.

NAME	AGE	OCCUPATION
James Weir	32	Baker
Richard C. Bonner	28	ex-NS Teacher
James McGahern	22	Car Driver
Patrick Cornyn	Unknown	Unknown
Joseph Gallagher	12	Scholar
Manus Craig	14	Farmer's Son
James Timoney	16	Farmer's Son
James McCallion	Unknown	Unknown
James Gorrell	28	Postman
Edward Melly	30	Farmer's Son
Francis McNeely	15	Butcher
Edward Doherty	26	General Dealer
Fergus Britton	21	Assistant Labourer
James McGettigan	19	Carpenter
Patrick Doherty	39	Butcher
Patrick Fox	30	Farm Labourer
William Lawn	31	Shop Assistant

Table 2: Balldeargs vs Bundoran, March 1906 (Camán).

THE FORMATION OF THE EAST AND WEST COUNTY BOARDS AND LEAGUE STRUCTURES

At the second meeting of the GAA county board, held on 10 November in Mountcharles, the camán league was formed. Two divisions were organised: Clann Dalaigh (from the Eany River to Bundoran) and Clann Suibhne (from the other side of the Eany River to Kilraine). The first camán fixtures were to take place on 26 November; Mountcharles were to play Donegal in the Clann Dalaigh division while Ardaghey were to take on Dunkineely in the Clann Suibhne section. Despite further communications of support from Letterkenny, Fintown, Ballinamore, Ardara, Glencolumbkille, Laghey, Glenties, Burt, Donegal and Ballyshannon, not everybody was supportive of the newly formed county board. Killybegs Emeralds manager Thomas Ward, having discussed the matter with his team, said his area was sticking to association football as they found the Irish game inferior.[85] Although Alfred C. Ward from Barnesmore was a member of the Mountcharles Coiste Ceanntair branch, he was adamant that people from his local district would not be participating in Gaelic games while 'certain individuals' were running the 'propaganda in this county'.[86]

On the morning of 24 November, the Derry-based newspaper reported on the first meeting of the east Donegal county board in Letterkenny, which was well attended. Vice-president Revd J.C. Cannon took the chair and the first draws for their football and hurling leagues were made; Gweedore and Burt Hibernians were selected to meet in the football, St Mura's of Fahan were drawn with Lámh Dearg from Letterkenny, and Newtoncunningham Harps received a bye.[87] These matches were played on St Stephen's Day in Letterkenny and were attended by Bishop O'Donnell, Very Revd Hugh Gallagher, president of St Eunan's Seminary, the Revd M.P. Ward and Revd J.C. Cannon, who presided over the meeting held in the reading rooms afterwards. Draws for the second rounds were made, and the secretary instructed to contact the Creeslough, Churchill and Glenswilly clubs regarding affiliation. Clubs in Inishowen were also to be contacted, and things looked bright for 1906.[88]

The Revd J.C. Cannon. (Courtesy of the National Library of Ireland)

Plate 10 Donegal GAA County Board West Division 1905-07 Participating Clubs

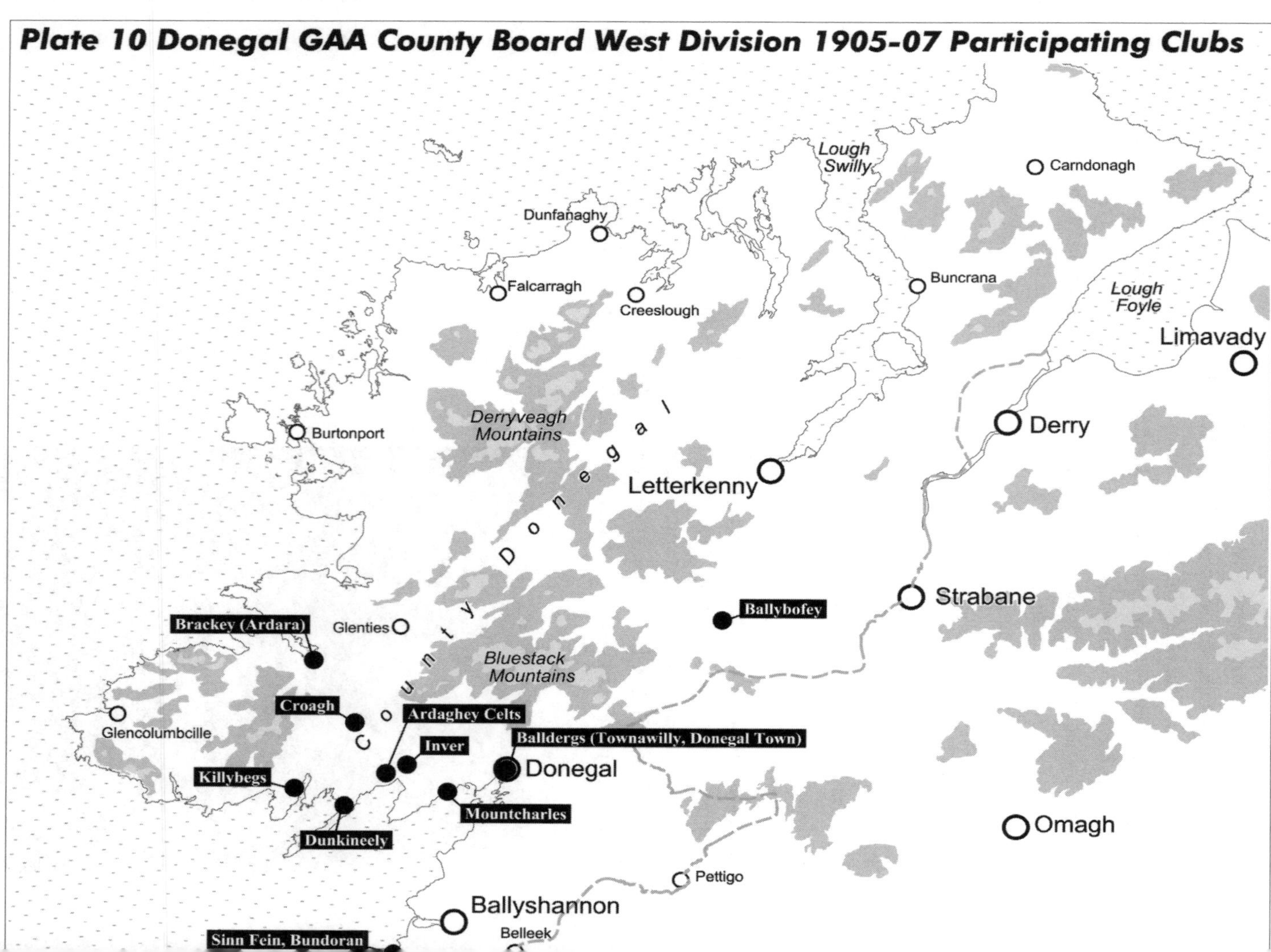

Plate 11 Donegal AA ounty Board East Division 1905-07 Participating Clubs

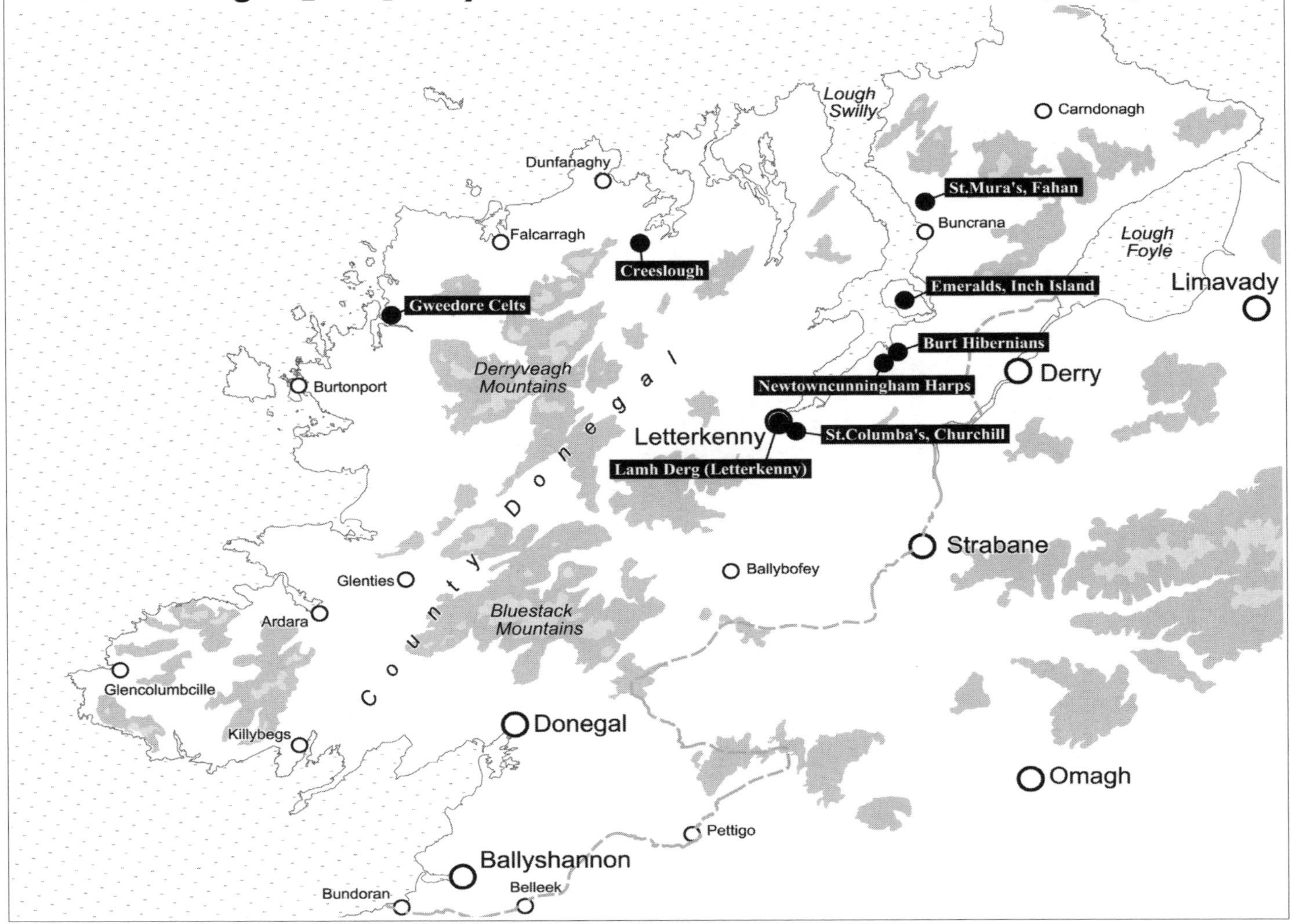

Lough Swilly
Carndonagh
Dunfanaghy
St.Mura's, Fahan
Buncrana
Falcarragh
Creeslough
Lough Foyle
Emeralds, Inch Island
Limavady
Gweedore Celts
Burt Hibernians
Derryveagh Mountains
Derry
Burtonport
Newtowncunningham Harps
Letterkenny
St.Columba's, Churchill
Lamh Derg (Letterkenny)
County Donegal
Strabane
Ballybofey
Glenties
Ardara
Bluestack Mountains
Glencolumbcille
Donegal
Killybegs
Omagh
Pettigo
Ballyshannon
Bundoran
Belleek

GROWTH OF GAA CLUBS WITHIN THE COUNTY

While the origins of the Burt Hibernians and Newtowncunningham Harps clubs can be traced to the late 1880s, the origins of St Mura's of Fahan and Gweedore Celts are unknown. St Mura's of Fahan had played a Christmas hurling match against Burt in 1899 and by 1903 were competing with this club in a hurling league organised by the Derry GAA. Gweedore Celts took part in a Gaelic League excursion to Doe Castle, where they defeated Clann Uladh of Derry in July 1906, which suggests that there was a strong Gaelic League influence in the club.[89]

Lámh Dearg of Letterkenny was founded on 18 September 1905 at a 'large and representative meeting' in the Literary Institute located in the centre of the town.[90] Shoemaker James Peoples, a member of the Irish National Federation and also of the United Irish League was elected president, and Bishop O'Donnell appointed patron. Patrick Sweeney was named captain, while merchant's son James McMonagle became vice-captain. Laurence Robbins, cashier in the Hibernian Bank Ltd, was appointed honourary secretary and auctioneer Patrick McFadden was named honourary treasurer.

Those present included a number of members of the Irish National Federation, and there were four Poor Law Guardians in attendance: town clerks Henry Gallagher and Patrick Doherty, John Campbell and Bernard Crampsie. Philip Hay, Superintendent of the Donegal District Asylum was also present, and this was significant as the club had his consent to play their matches on the local asylum grounds.[91] The club appears to have been able to conduct their affairs without any conflict with the local association football or cricket club.

The number of GAA clubs in Donegal increased gradually in 1906. In January, a GAA club was formed in Killygordon in the east of the county, and club officer Samuel Sexton thanked Seumas MacManus for his direction in organising this.[92] Officers were elected, including national school teacher P.A. Maguire, who became president, with James McGranahan named vice-president. Daniel Gallen was appointed secretary, while C.B. Duffy took on the secretarial duties.[93]

By April 1906, Creeslough and St Columba's of Churchill had joined the eastern division[94] and at the western division meeting the following month, proposals were made for a Gaelic football league to be started.[95] Five teams were affiliated, these being the Balldearg club, Bundoran, Mountcharles, Ballybofey and Killybegs. It was noted that Killybegs 'received a hearty welcome into the Gaelic ranks. Henceforth it cannot be said that the foreign game holds undisputed sway in Killybegs.'[96] These sniping comments were a recurring theme in the notes of the GAA in the local press around this time. Some GAA clubs were also eager to propagate the notion that they were growing in strength at the expense of association football. After the formation of the Mouncharles Gaelic football club in May 1906, it was reported:

> ... when Mountcharles took up the cause of the Gaelic games a portion of the young men had continued to play the game to which they were used – the Association game – but last week they properly and meritoriously resolved in a body to join with the other boys in their effort in propagating the Irish games.[97]

This enthusiasm for switching to Gaelic games was not the case in Killybegs, however. Of the Killybegs Emeralds team which won the Evans Cup in May 1906,[98] only three of these turned out for their local GAA club against Mountcharles at the end of the month.[99] Although players were known to switch codes in counties such as Westmeath at the beginning of the twentieth century,[100] both the majority of the Killybegs Emeralds and their Ardara namesakes remained focused primarily on the playing of soccer at this time.

FUNDING AND SUPPORT

The Ballybofey GAA club was also formed in May 1906, a month after a visit from the Balldearg camán team 'as a help towards getting a team started in that place'.[101] It was reported at their founding meeting that subscriptions would be taken in order to purchase the team kits and a challenge match was to be arranged against Strabane.[102] Other than club subscriptions, there is little evidence that these clubs benefited from local patrons, and this must have been a problem for them. However, a number of clubs were given permission from local farmers for the use of their fields. In 1906, the Balldearg club availed of a field given by local farmer Connell Cannon, a man described as 'a staunch supporter of every object pertaining to the welfare of Ireland' for their practice and matches.[103] Bundoran Sinn Féin GAA club were given the use of a field belonging to Mr Patrick Daniel Reavy, a veterinary surgeon, who was also their named their president in March 1906.[104] The Killygordon GAA club were able to rent 'a suitable field of play' from Mr John McNulty for the 1906 season.[105]

Attendance fees were evidently in use, particularly at camán matches in the north-east of the county, but with little coverage of clubs' financial progress in the local press it is difficult to establish how much support clubs received from the general public. The admission fee for the camán match between St Mura's of Fahan and Lámh Dearg of Letterkenny held in May 1906 was reportedly fixed at 3*d* with ladies being given free entry.[106]

The Sinn Féin Bundoran GAA club felt that admission fees were of a critical nature as 'expenses come rather heavily on a club, yet limited in numbers, so it is absolutely necessary that a nominal charge for admission should be made'.[107] Patrons were therefore encouraged to enter the ground properly, and the club also complained that after a camán match against Sligo opposition in December of 1906, 'the gate results were not at all in comparison with the huge crowd which assembled to witness the game'.[108] It is worth noting, however, that after the club's 1907 west Donegal camán final victory over Mountcharles, it was reported that, 'this victory is all the more creditable as the Bundoran team is quite young and has not received very much encouragement even at home'.[109]

While it is clear that the Donegal county board benefited from the support of Bishop O'Donnell in its early stages, the amount of financial support given to individual clubs is less easier to ascertain. However, there is some evidence of how they were able to sustain their activities. The members of the Mountcharles branch of Cumann na nGaedheal decided at their meeting in January 1906 that they would each pay 1*s* per month towards the travelling expenses of their camán team.[110] The Balldearg club received funds from a performance by their local drama club, but this was not a frequent means of supporting a GAA club at this time.[111] Mr Patrick Paul McConnell, manager of the local Hibernian Bank, donated a 'substantial subscription' to the Killygordon club, while the treasurer also received subscriptions of £4 in January 1906.[112]

Some matches were very well attended, judging by press reports, although these are of course only estimates. The 1906 replay of the west Donegal camán final between Ardaghey and Balldearg in July was apparently 'witnessed by hundreds of spectators on Mountcharles Strand',[113] while almost 2,000 spectators were said to have been present at a Gaelic football match between Gweedore Celts and Lámh Dearg in Gweedore the previous April.[114] Adverse weather conditions were sometimes highlighted as being a problem in attracting support, and given the climate in Donegal and without proper stands or covering, these must have been discouraging for spectators at times. A Gaelic athletic tournament held at the Asylum Grounds in Letterkenny on Easter Monday 1906, in which prizes were presented by Bishop O'Donnell, attracted only a small attendance. The 'very unfavourable' weather conditions undoubtedly contributed to this.[115]

Crowd behaviour at matches was generally excellent, if one is to believe the press reports, although it must be noted that some GAA writers were eager to portray a positive Gaelic atmosphere at their matches. At a camán match between Newtowncunningham Harps and the Grattan club of Derry held in April 1906, the reporter claimed that 'there was a vast crowd of spectators present. Where they came from puzzles me. Many of them must surely have come from distant places, nevertheless they were there, full of Gaelic enthusiasm, shouting encouragement and cheering for their countrymen.'[116] Female support did not go unnoticed, and the same reporter was eager to present the ladies in attendence as being 'typical daughters of Erin, rosy cheeked, part mouthed teeth as white as ivory, and black countenances, graceful figures, with innocent ways, and manners unsophisticated. They seemed to enter into the spirit of the game with quite as much spirit and zeal as their brothers.'[117] Crowd trouble appears to have been minimal around this time, although it was reported that at the initial west Donegal camán final in May 1906, 'the conduct of the spectators was not good at all, they being most of the time during the progress of the match on the ground of play, shouting in a frenzied manner'.[118] This appears to have been an isolated incident, however, and in comparison with crowd conduct in some Donegal FA matches in the 1890s, the behaviour of the crowd was not a problem for the GAA in Donegal in the period discussed in this chapter.[119]

Occasionally matches were advertised in the local press, most notably those in the north-east of the county. Excursion trains were sometimes granted for bigger attractions such as the aforementioned Grand Camán Parade, while three trains were organised for the camán final at the Aonach an Dúin Festival.[120]

CHAMPIONSHIP WINNERS

The progress of the Gaelic football leagues, or indeed the winners of the Gaelic football competitions, received little recognition in the local press. It appears that Lámh Dearg of Letterkenny won the Gaelic football championship of 1906 and that Balldearg of Donegal Town were victorious the following year, although there is evidence to suggest that this may have been the conclusion of the 1906 competition.[121] A Gaelic football match for medals was played at the Aonach an Dúin festival in July 1906 between selections representing both divisions, but the players and winners went unrecorded.[122] Whether the eastern Gaelic football champions ever took on the western winners is unclear. The failure of the western county board to secure a proper playing field for their final in 1906 and poor organisation meant that the matches between Balldearg and Mountcharles had to be abandoned, twice, owing to incursions of the tide.[123] It appears that this match was not rescheduled until May 1907.[124]

The same county board also had difficulty in deciding which camán team would face eastern winners Burt at the camán final for the Bishop's trophy at the Aonach an Dúin festival. Both the Balldearg and Ardaghey Old Celts teams had turned up hoping to play the decider for a place in the final after failing to resolve the affair within two matches, one of which involved a protest being lodged to the Ulster GAA Council.[125] However, there was not enough time to replay the match prior to the main event and it was decided that Ardaghey would go through after a toss of the coin by the Bishop himself.[126] It was here that the strong camán tradition of the Burt men became apparent, as they won easily. Ardaghey apparently struggled to adapt to grass, having previously played a number of games on sand, and the Bishop took the opportunity to praise the Christian virtues shown by the Burt team as he presented the cup to team captain George Dowds, who was a farmer from the townland of Moness.[127]

It is also possible to trace the socio-occupational status of the majority of Burt players around this time. The rural nature of the club is illustrated in the fact that the many players were general or agricultural labourers, while the Balldearg team consisted of a number of shop employees and labourers.

NAME	AGE	OCCUPATION
Jamie McLaughlin	38	General Labourer
James Gallagher	35	Railway Labourer
Charlie Dowds	34	Blacksmith
George Dowds	25	Farmer
John Gallagher	24	General Labourer
John Burns	29	General Farm Labourer
Willie Gallagher	29	Agricultural Labourer
John Whoriskey	27	Farm Servant
James Whoriskey	19	Unknown
Willie Kennedy	24	Farm Servant

Willie Moody	Unknown	Unknown
Tom Coyle	32	General Labourer
Manus Coyle	28	General Labourer
Willie Sheerin	Unknown	Unknown
Josie Campbell	34	Agricultural Labourer
Peter McCafferty	17	Unknown
John Moody	27	Farm Servant
John Griffin	24	Contractor
Hugh Doherty	25	Agricultural Labourer
Tom McCafferty	22	Labourer
John Deeney	21	Postman

Burt Hibernians, winners of the Bishop's Trophy at the Aonach an Dúin, 1906. (Courtesy of Damian Dowds)

Table 3: Burt Hibernians, 1906/7.

THE EVANS CUP, 1906

The Evans Cup competition began in February of 1906, over a year after it had been proposed. At the match between Killybegs Emeralds and their Ardara namesakes, played on 18 February, which ended in a 2-2 draw, Robert Evans himself was present, along with 'a very large number of spectators'.[128] The replay at the Owentocker valley ground in Ardara at the beginning of March was abandoned with twenty minutes to go, after a dispute, with Killybegs leading 1-0.[129] Killybegs won the replay after Ardara were fined £1 and it had been agreed that the referee would be from outside the local area. They then defeated the old Donegal Celtic (now playing under the name of Donegal United) in the final in Ardara at the end of April, with Charlie McIntyre and Tony Conwell scoring the decisive goals.[130] Some of these players were local tradesmen or fishermen, while a significant number were involved in the running of family businesses, which meant that they could avail of flexible hours to suit their sporting interests.

NAME	AGE	OCCUPATION
Joe McHugh	31	Postman
John Friel	21	Fisherman
Charlie Murrin	20	Assistant in family-run shop
Con Molloy	25	Barman/part of staff in Coane's Hotel
Johnny Dowds	23	Fisherman
Patrick Cunningham	21	Fisherman
Andrew McLoone	32	Assistant in family-run shop and hotel
Charlie McIntyre	25	Assistant in family-run shop
Charlie Green	20	Assistant in family-run shop
Edward Gallagher	25	Shop Assistant
Tony Conwell	23	Assistant in family-run shop
F McLoone	Unknown	Builder
Francis Cunningham	Unknown	Builder
Michael Boyle (management)	Unknown	Boatsman

Thomas A. Ward (manager)	26	Sales/Businessman
Hugh Duggan (management)	Unknown	Tea Agent
Dan Quigley (management)	25	Store Manager
John Ward (secretary)	33	Shop Assistant
Jim McGuire (management)	Unknown	Staff of Industrial School

Table 4: Killybegs Emeralds, 1906 Evans Cup winning squad and officials.

NAME	AGE	OCCUPATION
John Irwin	23	General Labourer
William Tierney	19	General Labourer
John McBrearty	26	Shop Assistant
Daniel McBrearty	26	Blacksmith
Patrick McDermott	36	Grocer
William McGroarty	Unknown	Unknown
Patrick McGowan	22	Shoemaker
Charles McBrearty	18	Unknown
John McGinty	27	Shoemaker
William Mullin	28	Stonemason
Patrick McGinty	22	Unknown

Table 5: Donegal United, 1906 Evans Cup final team.

Despite the initial success of the Balldeargs in the Donegal Town area, it is interesting to note that both shop assistant John McBrearty and shoemaker John McGinty appeared in the Donegal United cup final line-up and did not appear to take their job as GAA delegates too seriously. Both had been involved in their local soccer club for a number of years and were keen to continue.[131]

The delays between matches highlight the difficulties in organising competitive sporting matches in the area at the time. The Evans Cup committee did, however, seek to clarify their position on Gaelic games, and penned a long article in defence of their involvement in association football in the *Derry Journal* that April. They explained that a vote had been taken to play soccer for the 1906 season, but stated that the cup would be held under Gaelic football rules

Evans Cup Winners 1906, Killybegs Emeralds, pictured with the trophy. (Courtesy of Moira Mallon)

the following season. The writer listed their committee members as nationalists whom he claimed could 'be relied upon, without precipitate and fanatical action, [in] every necessary chance to further the national cause'.[132]

THE EVANS CUP, 1907

This is not to say that there was no GAA activity in Ardara, as there is evidence that there were two camán clubs operating in the parish at the time, although only one was affiliated to the west Donegal county board.[133] Plans to hold the soccer competition on a league basis were reconsidered at the first Evans Cup meeting in January 1907, but this proposal was scrapped, as it was feared that travelling expenses would be too high. This appears to be the reason why a number of soccer competitions in Donegal were not run on a league structure in the period covered in this book.

The cup committee made no mention of holding the tournament under any rules except those of association football, and seven teams, all from the south or south-west of the county, agreed to participate: Donegal, Ballyshannon, Killybegs, Clooney, Dungloe, Ardara Celtic and Emeralds.[134] The final was fixed for St Patrick's Day, but it was not until 23 June that the competition was decided, when Rosses Rovers from Dungloe took on Killybegs Emeralds at Sandfield. Despite the blustery conditions, there was huge interest in the final in the south-west area, 'as upwards of three thousand people witnessed the game'.[135] Robert Evans's father John kicked off the match, which the Dungloe men won 1-0. A friendly spirited function was held afterwards, with drinks being enjoyed from the cup, and hopes were expressed that the Evans family would return to stay in the Ardara area. However, this was to be the last final of the Evans Cup, as both association and Gaelic football competitions in Donegal had come to an end by the start of 1908.

THE DECLINE OF THE EVANS CUP

This decline in this soccer competition led to a letter in the *Derry Journal* being published in January 1908, in which 'A Kicker' enquired about what had become of the Evans Cup tournament.[136] This resulted in a number of sarcastic and belittling letters, which were published under pennames in the newspaper. One of these came from a correspondent writing under the penname of 'A Fair Player', claiming to be a committee member, who stated that, 'there were no entries for the cup this season, which goes to prove that competition under Association rules for this precious cup is a dead letter in south-west Donegal'.[137] He even went so far as to suggest that the cup should be raffled, with the proceeds being donated to charity. It is clear that the debate about the cup had certainly not been forgotten by those who had wanted to see it donated to the GAA. Despite further replies and debates nothing conclusive was decided.

There were branches of the United Irish League and the Ancient Order of Hibernians in Ardara at this time, and this may have influenced the decision not to host the 1908 competition. The final nail in the coffin of the Evans Cup came when the Ardara AOH, Division 107, at a meeting in the local hall on 10 May 1908, condemned the playing of soccer, as this was, they claimed, against their principles. The president, Brother Charles McGill, announced that their rules 'would have to be enforced, and strongly impressed on the members to be on their guard against being misled or hoaxed into any side issues by a combination of association footballers to suit their "own" game'. He also said that 'any attempt to lower the principles that we as Hibernians revere and foster, must be vigorously resisted by the Division'.[138] Although those present are not mentioned, in February 1907 a number of men such as Evans Cup secretary Michael McNelis, JP, and players Joseph McHugh, John Boyle, Charles Gildea and Peter Molloy were present at the Ardara division of the AOH's branch meeting, so it is quite possible that they were also part of the organisation the following year.[139]

In any event, it is clear that the cup committee were faced with some of the same difficulties as the Donegal FA had encountered in the 1890s; problems with transport, organisational difficulties and refereeing disputes were all evident. A month after the Ardara meeting, a letter appeared in the *Derry Journal* appealing to the Ulster branches of the AOH to be strong in their implementation of Irish culture. The writer claimed that the Irish Amateur Athletic Association had held a meeting in Belfast the previous week, 'and passed a resolution "warning off" all Irish athletes who compete in fixtures under the Gaelic Athletic Association'. He also stated that 'in Belfast, as well as in county Donegal, there are many professing Hibernians who are the backbone of the soccer code'.[140]

There was clearly much social and political pressure on these amateur sportsmen at the time, and, given these circumstances, it must have been very difficult to rebel against this. However, members of Donegal soccer clubs certainly partook in patriotic activities, such as song singing and recital, and of course would have seen themselves as nationalist and primarily Irish. After a friendly between Ballyshannon Ernes and Bundoran in November 1901, the post-match entertainment in Bundoran was predominantly nationalist, with Irish being spoken, and patriotic songs such as 'the Boys of Wexford' being 'rendered with vigour by all present'.[141]

It appears that before Seumas MacManus's campaign in 1905, there was little pressure on soccer clubs in the county to prove their allegiance to their country. Some players were indeed members of the Gaelic League, the AOH and the United Irish League. The idea of them being unpatriotic because they played what some perceived to be a 'foreign' and 'effeminate' sport was highlighted and propagated by fervent nationalists such as MacManus, members of the clergy and others in the Gaelic League through their writing and speeches. In truth, many were simply playing soccer for enjoyment and physical fitness, and in certain areas in Donegal Gaelic games had not been initiated into society and so association football was the only game available to them, and the rules, while not always clear cut, were better known than those used for Gaelic football.

In areas where the Gaelic League and its advocates were not strong enough, Gaelic games appeared to be slow to develop around this time. Certainly soccer was firmly established in the Inishowen peninsula and North-east of the county and those interested in maintaining their tradition were not easy to manipulate or indeed convert. At the beginning of the twentieth century, in smaller villages or towns, in a rural area, with the transport network in its infancy and with limited numbers of players available in the eighteen to thirty-five playing age group due to emigration, it was not always possible to join a club of another code outside one's own parish. If those responsible for organising sport in the area were predominantly interested in and knowledgeable about one code over another, then those interested in playing a team game would simply have had to stick with the preferred local sport if they wanted to stay in a sporting organisation, whether they favoured it or not. Therefore, Gaelic football clubs were always going to have difficulty competing with soccer clubs in these early days of the GAA in Donegal, as we shall see in the next chapter.

CONCLUSION

It is apparent that up until 1905 there was little pressure exerted on those who wanted to play association football in south Donegal. Seumas MacManus's campaign in the local press for an end to the playing of soccer was part of the growing awareness of the nationwide Gaelic revival, and there was a clear use of Gaelic games to promote an Irish identity different to that associated with perceived British pastimes. Mr MacManus's press appeal was boosted by a number of clergy of the Catholic Church, while Bishop O'Donnell also came out in support of Gaelic games, although it must be noted that he never criticised association football as harshly as other members of the clergy did at the time.

This nationalist movement was strongest in the Mountcharles and Donegal Town areas, and groups such as the Gaelic League, Cumann na nGaedheal and the Ancient Order of Hibernians were all involved in the promotion of what they perceived to be Ireland's national pastimes. The county's first association for Gaelic games was founded in October 1905, but not every soccer club in the south Donegal area was eager to follow their lead, and the transition to Gaelic games did not materialise as hoped at this time. The Evans Cup competition went ahead, with three local clubs taking part in 1906, and in 1907 the number of teams involved had more than doubled, with Erne FC from Ballyshannon also participating, although those attempting to run this competition were still suffering from political pressure in 1908 and it was not run again.

Gaelic games in Donegal were well publicised in the local press, and the Aonach an Dúin festival in 1906 saw the Burt club recognised as the outstanding camán club in the county. Camán seems to have been more popular in these years, but the competition with soccer would prove to be a major problem for the GAA. The other factors that curtailed the growth of Gaelic games in Donegal will be assessed in chapter four.

4

THE DECLINE OF THE DONEGAL GAA COUNTY BOARD AND THE DEVELOPMENT OF ASSOCIATION FOOTBALL IN SOUTH DONEGAL

'The [Carndonagh and Carrowmore] players were advised that they "should try to play the game with fewer soccer touches and endeavour to practice the distinctly Gaelic features".'[1]

LACK OF CO-OPERATION WITHIN THE DONEGAL GAA

Despite the apparent success of the camán final at the Aonach an Dúin festival in July 1906, it was clear that the Gaelic Athletic Association in the county was not developing as had been planned. At the October 1906 meeting of the western county board, with national school teacher Edward Daly of Bundoran in the chair, 'some comments were passed upon the non-attendance of delegates from the country'.[2] This absence, the six present believed, was because of the difficulty in attending Saturday meetings. It appears that those working on that day of the week could not get time off to attend. After arrangements were made for the previous season's football league final and the efforts of the Bundoran club remarked upon, it was decided that the camán league should go ahead, as Edward Melly of Donegal Town believed the sport was more popular in the county than Gaelic football, despite suggestions by the secretary that camán was a summer sport and football should be played in the winter.

However, more significantly, concerns were expressed about the lack of communication between the eastern committee and their own board, and it was decided that they should separate completely, as 'the present arrangement interfered more or less with freedom of movement'.[3] It was also stated 'that on every occasion a move was made by this side to fraternise with the eastern section their advances were either treated with contempt or totally disregarded'.[4] While the eastern county board still managed to organise a Gaelic Athletic tournament for St Stephen's Day, this lack of co-operation was hardly conducive to the growth of the association in the county. This event suggests a traditional support of Gaelic games around festival and holiday times at this stage, rather than a sustained organisation being in place. Only six teams were to be involved in this event, and Gweedore Celts and St Mary's of Fahan were no longer taking part.[5]

ATTEMPTS TO ORGANISE GAELIC FOOTBALL IN INISHOWEN

At the beginning of 1907, plans were being drawn up in the Carndonagh area in Inishowen for the playing of soccer to come to an end. The Gaelic League was active in that area at the time and at a meeting of local athletes held in the Carndonagh Temperance Hall on 5 January, 'it was proposed by the Revd Chairman, and seconded by G. Doherty, Carndonagh, "that the Gaelic football game be started and played throughout this district instead of the Association game, which has been played here for some time past"'. A match was organised for the following day and was begun by the Revd Father Mullin, CC, 'amid great applause'.[6]

The reporter also expressed hopes that other football clubs in the Inishowen area would take inspiration from this chain of events so that the sport would become widespread. By August of that year it was apparent that this changeover was not as simple as perhaps had been anticipated. At the Knockamany Sports, during the Inishowen Gaelic Festival, it was noted that teams from Carndonagh and Carrowmore (Culdaff) displayed 'a highly creditable' understanding of the rules and tactics associated with Gaelic football, considering 'Gaelic football has only been lately introduced into the peninsula'. However, the players were advised that they 'should try to play the game with fewer soccer touches and endeavour to practice the distinctly Gaelic features'.[7]

It is clear that there was a strong tradition of association football in the area and attempts at the eradication of the English sport never succeeded – it must be remembered that this area is situated close to Derry and, like west Donegal, many migrants to Scotland would have continued to play soccer on their return. Donal Campbell believes that by the time the Treaty port of Lough Swilly was taken over by the Irish Army in 1938, 'generations of Inishowen people had been lost to Gaelic games, soccer was the game of choice and – despite huge efforts – it was too late to bring these people back to Gaelic games'.[8]

DECLINE OF SUPPORT FROM THE CLERGY

The Fermanagh GAA county board illustrated the development of Gaelic games in their county by comparing their growth at that time with Donegal's decline in the *Donegal Independent* in February 1907,[9] and by April of 1907 the west Donegal county board were reduced to holding 'quarterly' meetings with the president, Revd Hugh Gallagher taking the chair, having replaced Revd Dr Maguire. It is evident that he was more interested in athletic competitions and encouraged these at this meeting.[10] Dr Maguire had become president of the newly opened St Eunan's College in Letterkenny and Revd Gallagher was clearly not as outspoken or influential regarding sporting matters as was his predecessor. It is apparent that club numbers did not rise sufficiently and there was not the same impetus by those who had been instrumental in the founding of the county board.

Both Revd Dr Maguire and Bishop O'Donnell seemed to have lessened their involvement in the Gaelic games movement in the county and were preoccupied with other interests. Dr Maguire's relocation meant that he was no longer living within the west Donegal county board area and was therefore less able to participate in its activities. More significantly, according to Dr Padraig Ó Baoighill in his biography of Cardinal O'Donnell, the GAA patron had fallen out with Gaelic League members around 1906 over funds[11] and was keen to stay loyal to the Irish Parliamentary Party.[12] This would partly explain why the Kilraine clergyman seems to have lessened his involvement with the GAA after 1906, and in any case, he was heavily involved in the promotion of other cultural interests such as the language question and education. Given MacManus's Sinn Féin links and O'Donnell's desire to see Home Rule, it is not difficult to ascertain that they may not have always agreed on certain matters. Ó Baoighill also states that leading members of the Gaelic League were absent at the Aonach in 1906[13] and despite the Bishop's hopes for the competition to be organised more effectively and continued for a number of years,[14] there was no mention of him being involved in the 1907 competition. It appears that the Gaelic football championship of that year was not completed.

DECLINE OF DONEGAL GAA ACTIVITY

The hurling championship was won by Sinn Féin of Bundoran, who defeated the holders Burt Hibernians in the final.[15] The Donegal GAA county board did, however, manage to organise a Gaelic Athletic tournament, which took place on 4 September 1907 in Donegal Town and was both well organised and attended.[16] This sports day consisted of a number of races and athletic events, but it was clear that the level of activity in Gaelic games had lessened dramatically at this stage and there were no county championships played from 1907 until 1919.

The July 1907 meeting of the Western county board appears to be the last one recorded in the local press and there is little evidence of any activity after this other than the aforementioned tournament in Donegal Town (and this was primarily an athletic event with the exception of a camán pucking competition).[17] The last eastern division activity recorded in the local press seems to have been the east Donegal camán cup match between Burt Hibernians and Newtoncunningham Harps in July 1907, and this Burt team went on to represent Donegal in the Ulster hurling final demolition of Antrim on 14 July in Burt.[18] Writing in *The Gaelic Athlete Annual and County Directory for 1907-8*, Cahir Healy, 'one of the founders of the Gaelic League and the GAA in Fermanagh',[19] claimed that Donegal 'seems to be asleep', although the county boards were still listed as being in operation, with their 1905 secretaries retaining their positions.[20]

SEUMAS MACMANUS'S EMIGRATION TO AMERICA

Clearly Seumas MacManus's aims from 1905 had not been accomplished at this point, and the reduction in his influence on sporting affairs may be partly explained by his frequent visits to America, where he would give lectures on Ireland and folktales.[21]

Writing in December 1906, in a letter from the office of *The Gaelic American* in New York to the Donegal Board of Guardians, he offered to resign from his post of Mountcharles division councillor and guardian, as he claimed that 'as he had been three months from the board, and as there was hardly any prospect of his returning for more than three months to come, he considered it was not right to deprive Mountcharles of its proper representation'.[22]

Although this resignation was not accepted, there is no doubt that his absence would have hugely affected his local community's nationalist and GAA activities. He was named president of the Donegal GAA county board in 1907,[23] but by November 1908 he had been made a Professor of Literature in the University of Notre Dame, where he had to take up office for a month each year.[24] In March 1911, it was reported in the local press that he had recently completed 'an extended lecturing tour over the United States –his fifth successful lecturing tour there'.[25]

MacManus's exile and his other interests would have meant he would have been unable to exert the same degree of activity in the organisation of Gaelic games as had been the case in 1905, while the Ethna Carberry branch of Cumann na nGaedheal's camán activities also seem to have deteriorated after the success of 1905/6. While there is little direct evidence that MacManus was financially supporting the GAA in Donegal at the time, it is not unrealistic to say that he may have, as he had previously donated to the Donegal Workhouse[26] and to the Mountcharles Gaelic classes.[27] Given the number of trips he made to America and his successful writing and lecturing abilities, he appears to have been in a sound financial condition around this time.

The AOH meeting of their Donegal county board took place on 15 December 1908 in the Hibernian Hall, Burtonport, where sixty-six divisions were represented.[28] Despite this large number of attendees, there was no mention of any type of sporting activity, and this was still the case almost nine months later at the Mountcharles AOH's meeting on 12 September 1909.[29]

DECLINE OF THE BALLDEARGS GAA CLUB

The decline of the Balldearg GAA club was highlighted in the Donegal Town notes of the *Donegal Independent* during 1907–8. The competition with the soccer club in the town was to prove more troublesome than they had anticipated and at one of their weekly meetings in February 1906, the club condemned the actions of an unnamed national school teacher who had encouraged a juvenile soccer match between Donegal and Ballyshannon teams. It was stated that 'the encouragement of foreign games by national teachers, in our opinions, will not conduce to the furthering of the Irish Ireland movement'.[30] At the end of October 1906, the club highlighted their struggle to displace association football, with farmer and club president Edward Melly and vice-president Michael Falconer appealing 'to all good

Irishmen and Irishwomen to give their undivided support to the games and pastimes of Ireland, and to relegate once and for all those of the foreigner'.[31] They also claimed that they had faced 'bitter opposition' from those whom they had expected to give their undivided support.[32]

In mid-December, their Gaelic football team again had to abandon their west division final against Mountcharles on the Holmes' Strand, after the tide once again interrupted the action. While it is not clear when this game was finally decided, it appears they were declared 1906 champions.[33]

With the deterioration of GAA activity in 1907, the Balldearg club members faced some harsh criticism in the *Donegal Vindicator* for their apparent inactivity and disloyalty to their primary sports. In February 1907, the writer of the Donegal Town notes complained that Balldearg were 'tottering to their fall' and that 'it is difficult to remedy any matter when and where an ardent willingness does not prevail'.[34] He also claimed that 'so called prominent hurlers' were attending 'the games of the Sassenach'.[35] At the Evans Cup match between Donegal Celtic and Killybegs on 10 March, 'out and out Gaelic Leaguers so dubbed' were present and 'cheered vociferously for the Celtic team, indicative most certainly that they were in full accord that day with foreign imitations'.[36]

It appears that the nationalist spirit which prevailed in the area during 1905 had gone into decline, and some people felt that strict adherence to the promotion of and dedication to Gaelic games wasn't always significant enough or necessary to keep them away from other forms of sporting entertainment. Indeed, with the lack of general entertainment available in Donegal society at the time, it was a big ask for the GAA to expect young men to stay away from soccer. Despite P.M. Gallagher's involvement in a number of Gaelic athletic tournaments held in July and September, the decline of the west Donegal GAA county board did little to help the club's stability. Arrangements had been made at the July meeting held in Mountcharles for a Gaelic football league to be started and for the purchase of a cup, but there is little evidence that this was followed up.[37] Hurling trainer, player and IRB suspect Richard C. Bonner had moved to Glasgow by May 1908[38] and given his involvement in the club and in the running of Gaelic games in the area, his loss would have been comparable to that of Seumas MacManus.

At the end of July 1908, cricket was apparently being played again in Donegal Town,[39] and a week later one writer highlighted the Balldeargs' decline:

> Did the Donegal hurling club make their final appearance some weeks ago when they travelled to Bundoran and suffered such ignominous defeat at the hands of

> the team there? If so, it seems a pity they did not give their fellow townsmen an inkling of this to enable them to witness their last exhibition and if possible a memento of their retirement, should it only be a lock of their hair.'[40]

He also questioned their players' allegiance to their native pastimes and went so far as to suggest that they were receiving payment for playing cricket:

> ...we noticed a number of the players were one time prominent hurlers and Gaelic footballers. The only reason that can be assigned for this sudden 'turn of their coats' is that they must belong to the class of young men who go with the wind without any respect for principle, their principle being – what pays best.[41]

This type of journalism echoed that identified in County Westmeath around 1905 by Tom Hunt, where 'activities and events inherent in soccer and cricket were condemned as promoting notions of servility, subjection and allegiance to the alien power in Ireland'.[42]

By October 1908, it was claimed in the *Donegal Independent* that as local GAA matches and practices were 'a thing of the past, it was taken for granted that the club had dissolved or "extinguished". It therefore came as a surprise to find that the weekly meetings are still being held though for what purpose it is impossible to tell.'[43] Handball fixtures took place between the Donegal club and Drimarone in August 1908, but it was clear that soccer and cricket were most prominent in the town, despite strong attacks and accusations of drunkenness in the local press at this time.

THE ULSTER GAA COUNCIL

Problems with administration were evident at the Ulster GAA's provincial meeting that was held in Strabane at the beginning of December 1908. Although this appears to have been only a branch meeting, it is clear from this episode that soccer was not the only sport which suffered from organisational and ruling difficulties. At the meeting, which took place in the Gaelic League Rooms, Barrack Street, Strabane, on 6 December, Donegal was represented by John Dowds from Burt, and Daniel O'Doherty from Strabane took the chair.

Donegal had been defeated by Derry in the Ulster hurling championship on 15 November in Burt and this game was not without controversy:[44]

> In this appeal Donegal alleged the illegal constitution of the Derry team, in as much as one of the players (Peter McCallion) was a resident in Donegal, and another (Harry Coyle) was under suspension. Six other points alleging infringements of the rules during the progress of the match were also appended.[45]

After the report of the referee, Con O'Regan from Belfast, was read, along with correspondence from the Derry and Donegal County Committees, a letter from George Martin, provincial secretary, was heard. He claimed that, 'although the Donegal appeal had been lodged with him within the proper time, the stipulated fee which must accompany each appeal was not received within the specified limit'.[46] It was decided that the appeal would be rejected, as in future other teams who had not sent the appropriate fee would not pay if they lost the decisions. 'Mr Dowds explained the cause of delay in forwarding [the] full fee, pointing out the difficulties in procuring postal orders and the uncertain mail deliveries in country districts.'[47] However, the chairman Mr O'Doherty declared the appeal void and Derry were awarded the victory. This was not the end of the unsavoury feelings at the meeting, and the role of the Ulster Council was strongly condemned by the Derry, Tyrone and Donegal officials regarding the selection of venues for meetings, as none of their counties had hosted an Ulster Council gathering in three years.[48]

This sense of isolation from the province's governing body in Gaelic games undoubtedly contributed to the decline of the association in these years in Donegal, and, as illustrated by John Dowds, means of communication were not very reliable in certain places at the time. At the Ulster GAA Provincial Council's Annual Convention, which was held in the Hibernian Hall in Clones at the beginning of February 1909 under the presidency of Patrick Whelan, Donegal's late fee was ordered to be refunded, but perhaps more significantly they were the only Ulster team not included in the first round of the Ulster Gaelic football championship. Although both Donegal GAA county boards had appointed delegates to the Ulster Council in 1905, little has been recorded of their participation, although *Sport* noted the election of the Revd J.C. Cannon as vice-president in January 1907[49] while Balldearg members Messrs Crawford and Cornyn were in attendance at the June 1906 meeting held in Clones.[50] It is difficult, therefore, to establish how much encouragement the Ulster GAA Council gave to Gaelic games in Donegal without evidence of surviving minutes, which are unavailable prior to 1917.

PLAYING OF ASSOCIATION FOOTBALL AGAIN UNCHALLENGED IN SOUTH DONEGAL

There was an unquestionable revival in soccer activity throughout Donegal in 1909, most notably along the west coast, where clubs such as Rosses Rovers and Gweedore Celtic were reorganised. However, there were no cup competitions held, despite a letter to the *Derry Journal* published on 31 March from 'A Donegal Footballer' appealing for competitive soccer in the county to be relaunched.[51] This time there was no reply from any sporting body. Soccer was now being played again without obstruction in south Donegal, and Glenties United and Ardara took part in a challenge match on 20 April at Tullyhonevet in Glenties before 'a very large crowd of spectators'.[52] The annual Cranford athletic sports and athletic races, held on 29 July, were attended by the band of the Golan AOH, who 'discoursed a selection of national and patriotic airs during the day to the great delight of the crowd assembled'.[53] It was claimed that this crowd of 'several thousand' people was the biggest seen in over twenty-five years of the event, which was described as 'the premier sports in North-west Donegal'.[54]

THE TEMPERANCE MOVEMENT IN DONEGAL

Soccer was the preferred type of football in the Cranford area, and the competition was run along 'strictly temperance lines, not a trace of intoxicating drink being allowed to enter the park'.[55] It appears that many sporting clubs and organisations were teetotal around this time. Although Neal Garnham believes that 'various elements of the vibrant temperance movement' could lead to the founding of soccer clubs,[56] there is little evidence to suggest that this was the case in Donegal. There is some evidence, however, to suggest clubs' involvement in the temperance movement, with the aforementioned Cranford team in 1895, and Diarmaid Ferriter claims that 'temperance entered the wider lexicon of Irish cultural progress in the opening years of the century, a revival of the nineteenth-century idea that "Ireland sober" would be Ireland free'.[57] After the postponement of a friendly match between Rashedog Rovers and Breenagh from Glenswilly (outside Letterkenny) in February 1909, the *Derry Journal* reported that the parties involved travelled to the nearby Temperance Hall of P. McGinley, where lunch was served and they played billiards, with dancing and singing to the piano and violin also taking place.[58]

In a letter to the *Derry Journal* about the forthcoming Feis Tír Conaill, which was to be held in Doe Castle near Creeslough on 29 June 1910 and presided over by Bishop O'Donnell, patrons were reminded by the organisers that the ideals of the temperance movement were to be observed, 'as the promotion of temperance among our people is one of the foremost purposes of the Irish Revival Movement'.[59] While there is no mention of any sport at the event, it is clear that there was a strong drive by the Catholic clergy to promote the abstinence from alcohol in Donegal society, and Canon McFadden was again involved in this. On 10 July 1910, he presided over the first meeting of the Glenties Temperance Society, which was held in the local parochial hall.[60] On 2 August, the newly formed society, numbering almost 1,500 people, travelled to Letterkenny for their excursion as had been planned at the meeting. They were met by the local band and by Monsignor McGlynn and Fr McCafferty, who accompanied them to the Bishop's residence, where he welcomed them. The Glenties and Fintown bands were present under the banners of the AOH divisions and a number of sports events took place, 'the Glenties (Gortnasillagh) tug-of-war team defeated Letterkenny, and in the football match (Gaelic) the honours were about equally divided. Other sports followed, and everybody returned highly pleased at the day's entertainment.'[61] The congregation also visited St Eunan's College and the Cathedral.

GAELIC GAMES AND ASSOCIATION FOOTBALL IN BALLYSHANNNON

With the domination of association football and cricket in Ballyshannon at the turn of the twentieth century, Gaelic games did not get an opportunity to flourish in the town, although a hurling club had been formed in 1904. The club, known as the O'Donnells, played what was thought to be the first hurling match in the town 'within living memory' on Easter Monday 1904, against Enniskillen at the Rock enclosure.[62] Despite the hosting of céilís, one of which was 'well filled, principally by the members of the Ballyshannon, Bundoran and Belleek branches of the Gaelic League', and the publishing of hurling phrases in the local press, the club struggled to gain a foothold in the area.[63] Proposals to start a Gaelic football team were discussed at the hurlers' meeting on 12 February 1905, but by the time the Donegal county board was founded in October 1905, it was clear that these plans were proving difficult to implement in the town.[64]

P.A. Mooney. (Courtesy of the National Library of Ireland)

The *Donegal Vindicator* felt that the slow development of the Gaelic League in the town was due to the local businessmen and professionals who failed to show sufficient interest in the Ballyshannon branch, and claimed that part of the blame lay with *Donegal Independent* editor P.A. Mooney, whom they felt, despite his new role as vice-president of the county GAA committee and Ulster Council delegate, had done little to promote the Gaelic League in his newspaper. Again, this is evidence of the partiality of the press during this era and these two Ballyshannon newspapers were not always working in harmony with each other. The *Donegal Vindicator* also encouraged 'every man in town worth his salt' to join the league, but there was also sufficient competition from the Erne Football Club, now competing in the IFA Junior Cup, to ensure that association football was to the fore in the town at the time.[65]

ERNE FOOTBALL CLUB AND THE IFA JUNIOR CUP

The club had started the season by affiliating to the North-west Football Association and organised a raffle for a 'beautiful eight day clock' and a pipe, which were put on display at Mr Sweeny's White Horse Bar.[66] The Donegal–Ballyshannon Railway extension meant greater ease of travel, and the club made sure their matches were well publicised both in the local press and by putting up posters in the town.[67] They also leased a pitch for the season from Mr Cummins.[68]

The IFA Junior Cup was a competition for teams 'whose players were not considered of a high enough standard to compete in the Irish cup proper'.[69] Having defeated Donegal Celtic in the first round of this competition in their first ever match for 'outside honours' in October 1905,[70] Erne progressed to meet Omagh United in Tyrone. The *Donegal Vindicator* chronicled the club's resurgence and claimed that the team had been put through 'a course of hard training' since their defeat of their local rivals. The event was highlighted with a team photograph in the paper before the game, a fairly uncommon occurrence in the local Donegal press and normally reserved for the achievements or deaths of the local clergy at the time.

The Ernesiders were not favoured to make much progress as the Omagh team was so far undefeated that season and 163 teams had initially entered the competition.[71] This match, played on Saturday 10 November, will go down as the high point in the club's history and it was reported that 'after ninety minutes brilliant and dashing play the Ernes won the best match they have ever played by the score of one goal to nil'.[72]

Arriving on the midday train from Ballyshannon after a ninety-minute journey, the team 'having got into their colours made their way to the field where they were well received'.[73] Fleming's scrappy first-half goal was the culmination of a spell of pressure by the away team, and despite relentless attacking from the Omagh men in the second-half, 'McAllister and Kelly were an impregnable pair of backs – a barrier that was hard to pass – but occasionally Omagh got by and then McIntyre had to save his side.'[74] The *Ulster Herald* described it 'as undoubtedly the best match played at Omagh this season' and claimed that 'the enthusiasm amongst the spectators went to a great pitch … in some instances the language indulged in was entirely out of place'.[75] After the match, the Ernes were entertained by the home team before being seen off at the train station by a number of Ballyshannon men who were living in Omagh.[76]

Disappointingly for the Erne club, they were drawn away to Strabane Celtic in the third round and this was seen as regrettable, because of 'the weak financial situation of the club' and the fact that they would have to 'bear the expenses of a second trip'.[77] As it happened, they did not make it past their Tyrone opponents on this occasion, going down by four goals to one.[78] Despite proposals by the IFA in September 1906 to extend the playing area of the Fermanagh and Tyrone Football Association to include teams from Sligo, Donegal and Leitrim, and a grant of £50 being given 'to combat Gaelic football in the districts mentioned'[79] there is no evidence to suggest that Erne FC benefited in any way or participated in this competition.

This financial strife was not conducive to the club's provincial development and they returned to playing Donegal opposition, winning the Woods Cup which was organised in 1909. The club apparently even tinkered with the idea of switching to Gaelic games in 1906, but this proposal came to no avail and there was no affiliation with the short-lived Donegal GAA organisation.[80]

ATTEMPTS TO REVIVE THE GAA IN DONEGAL

It was, however, the Gaelic League who were responsible for the foundation of the Aodh Ruadh GAA club which was formed in the Rock Hall in Ballyshannon at the end of October 1909 with the promise of Denis Nyhan, one of the founder members of the Erne soccer club, that a silver cup would be offered for football competition.[81] While it is obvious that serious efforts to encourage the playing of Gaelic football throughout the county had ground to a halt by this time, the members of the Ballyshannon Gaelic League had decided to hold a meeting on 21 October to revive the Irish games after a proposal by farm labourer John McCormack. They felt there had been 'no outdoor amusement of any kind in Ballyshannon' over the previous few years and were eager to do something for the winter.[82]

Competitions in Gaelic games in Donegal were limited to local areas for a number of years after the decline of the GAA county championships, although the Aodh Ruadh club was instrumental in organising a hurling competition named the Assaroe Cup during 1911. This was a cup donated by Henry J. Toal, IRO, and at the club's AGM on Sunday 9 October he decided that, although the cup had initially been offered for Gaelic football in April, to use it for hurling purposes, as there were 'very few Gaelic football clubs in the county … and there being no teams within a reasonable travelling distance the idea had to be abandoned'.[83] The hurling final was played in June 1911 in Letterkenny – local team Tír Conaill were defeated in the final by Lámh Dearg from Derry.[84]

The Aodh Ruadh hurling club also held their annual athletic sports that month and received a cup from J.J. Woods of the Mall Bar, who was keen to promote all local sports, for their marathon race.[85] Despite the club's links with the Gaelic League, it is interesting to note that they denied any involvement in boycotting association football and welcomed all new members, claiming, 'we wish to play our own game without interfering with anyone'.[86] The club also held debates on Gaelic matters and encouraged their members to join this organisation, but appeared comfortable with other sports being played in the area at the time.[87]

At the Feis Tír Conaill, which was held in Donegal Town on 29 June, Ardaghey took on Letterkenny in a hurling match which was won by the former. It was reported that, 'the Letterkenny club has come into existence only recently and the Ardaghey team … has been reorganised only a short time ago by the Revd James J. Brennan, CC Inver, a man who is always in the forefront of the Irish–Ireland movement'.[88]

Despite the decline in the playing of Gaelic football, hurling was still being played in certain areas in Donegal, and in August there was a large attendance at a Junior League competition which was held by the Tír Conaill hurling club in Letterkenny. Faugh-A-Ballagh defeated Eire Óg to claim a set of silver medals donated by the home club.[89]

Tír Conaill's proposal to donate a silver cup for a Gaelic football county championship and divide the county into two divisions in November of that year attracted little support.[90] This illustrates the lack of interest in Gaelic games in the county at this time, when the majority of the clubs which had been prominent in the 1905 county board seem to have been disbanded.

Aodh Ruadh noted at their AGM in October that hurling practices were more prominent in their club, claiming that, 'this is owing to so very few Gaelic football clubs being in the neighbourhood'.[91] Hurling was also being played in Bundoran around this time and the revival of their club, the Pioneers TA, was illustrated in the *Donegal Independent* on 16 February 1912. In a short report which chartered their decline since 1907, it was claimed that they now had 'as good, if not a superior, team to the much boomed Sinn Féiners who had won the county championship in 1907'.[92]

At the AGM of the Aodh Ruadh club in November 1912, some of the difficulties which the Ballyshannon club faced were discussed – emigration was a big problem as this caused the club to lose 'many of its most prominent members' and they had to abandon their plans for their annual Gaelic sports as they couldn't get a suitable field for the event. They also temporarily lost their training field, but were gaining new members and were supported by the De La Salle Brothers, who helped to set up a junior hurling team in connection with the club. The club held several balls which were well patronised and the dance classes they had set up for the winter increased funding and provided a source of amusement.[93] However, it appears they were reduced to playing local teams in friendly matches as there were no further Donegal hurling county championships played until the 1920s.

The County Donegal tug of war team, 1897. J.J. Woods is first left, back row. (Courtesy of the British Library)

THE WOODS CUP

Association football continued to be played in Ballyshannon, and the Woods Cup competition was organised in November 1909. J.J. Woods was a Mayo man who, while serving in the RIC in 1897, had competed in the shot put at the North-west Constabulary Sports in Derry on 22 May of that year[94] and had also been part of the County Donegal tug-of-war team which won the silver medal that day.[95] He had retired from the force in October 1904 after twelve and a half years' service, and this was marked with a Smoking Concert held in the Stag's Head Restaurant, Derry, where he was presented with 'a very handsome marble clock by the men of Victoria station'.[96] On Sunday 30 October 1904, he married Miss O'Dowd of the Mall. He was clearly a popular man in Ballyshannon and it appears he took over the local Mall Bar.[97]

POOR BEHAVIOUR OF PLAYERS AT THE WOODS CUP

The cup committee met initially on Friday 19 November 1909, and the proposed rules were submitted and passed. General clerk James Byrne was elected secretary with Mr Bamford presiding. Woods himself took up the position of treasurer, while coach maker Denis McGuire was moved to the chair.[98] The draw was made at the Erne FC rooms on 13 December, with seven teams involved: Ernes, Bundoran, Killybegs, Dunmuckram, Belleek (Fermanagh), Cliffoney (Sligo), Killybegs and Manorhamilton (Leitrim).[99] While the Bundoran, Sligo, Leitrim and Fermanagh teams were all located a short distance from Ballyshannon, Killybegs was about twenty-five miles away (but on the train line).

The tournament did not get off to a good start, with a number of teams walking off during the opening matches. This lack of discipline led to the committee issuing a warning to clubs in the *Donegal Vindicator*. Supporters and players were ask to note that the competition, 'was not intended as a competition for the best exhibition of rowdyism, or for the best fighting men in the counties of Donegal, Fermanagh and Leitrim, but as a source of season's amusement for young people in association football'.[100] It was also claimed that 'the playground at each match is turned into a veritable battle field where the opposing teams charge each other seemingly intent on doing bodily harm'.[101] Players and spectators were also advised that the referee's word 'should be a law' and 'older and wiser spectators' were asked to condemn those who made life difficult for the official – mainly 'a rabble of young lads'.[102]

Teams were also advised to play to the whistle and continue after the referee's decision had been made, otherwise the competition was in danger of collapsing into oblivion.[103] Clearly there were problems with interpretation of the rules, and the lack of available neutral referees was also apparent. While this was not the end of the unrest on the field, Erne FC were later declared competition winners and their team photograph was put on display in Gas Works' manager William Millar's shop on the main street. Cliffoney received the runners-up medals.[104]

The 1910/11 tournament went ahead the following winter, with Donegal Celtic victorious but receiving little credit in the *Vindicator* for their achievement. Given that the newspaper was printed in Ballyshannon and that the cup received little coverage in the other local papers, it is difficult at times to gain a neutral perspective on these games.[105] It is possible, however, to identify a number of their players from a match against Cliffoney in February 1911. A number of these were employed in shops within the town and all were relatively young, although Patrick McGowan was the only remaining player from the 1906 team.

NAME	AGE	OCCUPATION
John Farrell	21	Railway Shunter
Bernard McGinty	22	Draper's Assistant
William McGlanaghy	21	General Labourer
Joseph McGlanaghy	19	Boat and Shoemaker
William Crawford	21	Fisherman
Charles Martin	19	Shop Assistant
Eddie Doherty	31	Merchant/Dealer
Edward Cassidy	26	Farm worker
J. Brogan	Unknown	Unknown
Patrick McBrearty	22	Solicitor's General Clerk
Patrick McGowan	27	Boot & Shoemaker

Table 6: Donegal Celtic, 1911.

At the October 1911 meeting, a council for the forthcoming tournament was elected and the rules were revised. Among these was the extension of the area for competing teams to thirty miles; objections were to be overlooked until the semi-final stage and the idea of a Charity cup was discussed.[106] In December, Killybegs Emeralds defeated the holders, Donegal Celtic, by 2-1 in 'showery weather before a fair attendance'.[107] According to Neal Garnham, 'crowd problems at matches in Belfast reached a hiatus in the two years before the outbreak of the Great War',[108] which led to Irish Football League clubs such as Glentoran distributing handbills which condemned crowd disorder.

Although there is some evidence of crowd trouble experienced by the Donegal FA in the 1890s,[109] and the Woods Cup committee had to contend with the aforementioned problems during its initial season, there does not appear to have been anything as serious as the incident which occurred in a match between Donegal and Ballyshannon in January 1912. A Donegal player had his right ear 'severely bitten' and he was also kicked in the eye by his Ballyshannon opponent. It is not clear if this was a Woods' Cup match although these teams were certainly involved in this competition at the time. The game was played in Ballyshannon and it was reported that the injury took place after 'a quarrel arose between supporters of the combatants, which resulted in fisticuffs'. It is evident that there was a strong rivalry between the sides, 'There was a large crowd of spectators present, and angry words took place between the "locals" and the visitors, everything at one time pointing to a row that would have been difficult to quell, and ont [sic] of which the consequences were certain to be grave.'[110]

ARDARA EMERALDS' FUTURE GAA PLAYERS

Despite the fact that the Ardara Emeralds team were no longer involved in competition (the lack of a direct train line into the town would have hampered their chances of taking part in the Woods Cup) it is possible to identify those who were part of the team in 1912, and a number of these would go on to play prominent roles in the GAA club founded there in 1921. Goalkeeper John Maloney, a farmer from Brackey, starred in Ardara's first county championship win in 1923, along with wool carder Charlie Gallagher, while national school teacher Seán Ó Casaide went on to train the team and later became secretary of the Donegal GAA county board. The following is a profile of the 1912 soccer team members identified from a photograph.

NAME	ADDRESS	AGE	OCCUPATION
Johnnie Boyle	Main Street	31	Flesher
Tommy Maguire	Main Street	23	Bookkeeper
John Maloney	Brackey	32	Farmer
James Cannon	The Diamond	33	Cooper
Johnny Maguire	Main Street	27	Postman
Peter Breslin	Drumbarron	23	Baker
Barney Boyle	Main Street	26	Butcher
John Cassidy	The Diamond	25	N.S. Teacher
Richard Howley	Drimaha	16	Scholar
Francis Maguire	Main Street	21	Scholar
Charlie McCaul	The Diamond	28	Farm Manager
Charlie Gallagher	Front Street	22	Wool Carder

Table 7: Ardara Emeralds, 1912.

Ardara Emeralds FC, 1912. (Courtesy of John McConnell)

Killybegs Emeralds FC, 1911. (Courtesy of Moira Mallon)

THE WOODS CUP FINAL 1912

In 1912, the ever improving Killybegs Emeralds team progressed through to the Woods Cup final after a series of league matches. The ports of Killybegs and Ballyshannon had important trading links; ships were unable to dock in Ballyshannon so Killybegs was used for this purpose, with a number of Ballyshannon merchants storing their goods in warehouses in Killybegs before their transferral via the rail network.[111]

The deciding fixture was played on Easter Monday, 8 April, against Ernes, who were also joint top of the table. The Donegal Railway Company were happy to oblige with transport by putting on a special train from the south-west village, despite the coal strike which prevailed at the time, with the return fare fixed at half a crown.[112]

The match was held in Ballyshannon and 'the weather conditions were unfavourable, but a fair crowd turned out to witness the game'.[113] Killybegs were victorious by 3-1 and Tony Conwell received the cup from the president of the Woods' Cup Council, Denis McGuire. Having thanked the cup committee on the way the competition was run, the shop assistant and captain 'said it was one of the happiest days of his life'.[114] The Killybegs team returned home, 'where they were met by a large contingent and a procession was formed, headed by the football club, and [they] marched to the Foresters' Hall, where a most enjoyable night's dancing was held. The town was beautifully illuminated in honour of the occasion.'[115]

DECLINE OF ASSOCIATION FOOTBALL COMPETITIONS IN BALLYSHANNON

On 25 October 1912, the *Donegal Independent* advertised the forthcoming Woods Cup and also the Charity Cup, which was donated by publican Edward Rogers and to be contested in the same area as the Woods Cup.[116] There was very little recorded in the local papers about the Woods tournament in 1913, but a report in the *Donegal Independent* highlighted similar problems to those encountered by the Donegal FA in the 1890s. A letter written by 'An Onlooker' highlighted the fact that the Belleek players involved in a Woods Cup match against Erne Celtic were not all from the Belleek area and he called for the Woods Cup Council 'to take the necessary steps to guard the interests of their clubs and supporters'.[117]

Fermanagh side Belleek Rose Isle won the Woods Cup in 1913[118] and the Charity Cup final between Belleek and Ballintra was played on Easter Monday and resulted in a scoreless draw. This time there were complaints that Ballintra were using players from outside their area, as 'A Pottery Supporter' illustrated, 'Belleek excelled itself. We knew they could play football, but never expected them to put up such a fight against Ballyshannon, Donegal, Derry and Strabane, with a small sprinkling of Ballintra thrown in.'[119]

The *Donegal Independent* reporter who covered the game was unhappy with the admission fee and the absence of any female supporters. He posed the question, 'had "ladies must pay" anything to do with this?' and complained that an hour was too short 'for an international entrance fee'.[120]

The replay, which was played on 6 April, was highly controversial and it appears the conduct of the Belleek players was far from satisfactory. The referee was struck before the match took place and the crowd invaded the field during the game. Although no scoreline is given, it seems that Belleek won the match, and Hugh Deery, Ballintra, wrote a 'strongly worded' report condemning the Beleek players' conduct. The *Donegal Independent* would not publish the report in full and the editor claimed that they didn't want anything further to do with local football.[121]

Neither the Woods nor Charity Cups were held in the 1913/14 season. In March 1913, Erne FC withdrew from both the Woods and Charity Cup competitions[122] and it appears the club did not have the enthusiasm to help organise a competition for the following season.

However, it was not the end of cup soccer in south Donegal. In the autumn of 1913 the Britton Cup, a tournament organised by Donegal Football Club, was underway, with Ballybofey availing of the railway system to travel into south Donegal to challenge Ballyshannon United, Killybegs, Donegal and Drimarone on a league basis.[123] The Britton Cup was donated by Donegal Town watchmaker and jeweller William Britton, and the competition saw rivalry between the Donegal Town and Ballyshannon teams reach a new high. Despite topping the table in mid-December,[124] as the tournament moved into its second round in the New Year the Ballyshannon men seemed to self-destruct during their home game against Donegal FC on Sunday 25 January. The referee, Patrick McDermott, a Donegal Town shopkeeper who had associations with his local club, was struck by two of the Ballyshannon players.[125] Mr McDermott awarded the game to Donegal and had to be escorted from the field by members of the cup committee as, he claimed, a crowd of 'about 300 people', having invaded the pitch, surrounded him.[126]

Again the lack of discipline amongst players and spectators during local football at the time was evident, and the referee claimed in his report that 'we were followed by a crowd of hooligans, shouting, roaring, calling filthy remarks, throwing and kicking stones and sods at us in this manner up to McGurren's in Back Street'.[127] He asked the cup committee to suspend a number of the Ballyshannon players and requested that the club's ground be closed for matches until 1 May.[128] These events arose when he disallowed a Ballyshannon goal and shortly afterwards allowed a Donegal Town effort to stand. The Ballyshannon club complained bitterly and their protest was made up of five points, one of which being that the referee had failed to condone a Donegal player who was wearing hobnailed boots. The other points centred on the offside rule and they asked the cup council to award them the points.[129]

Given the controversies which continue to arise in professional football today, despite modern technology and clearer understanding of the rules, it is not hard to understand why the problems which plagued local Donegal soccer in the opening decade of the twentieth century were not easy to rectify. The *Donegal Independent* naturally defended their home club and, while admitting that the behaviour of 'a couple of players and spectators was … deserving of the utmost censure', contradicted the referee and claimed his statement was 'astounding'.[130]

They also published their report of the South Donegal Football League, whose meeting was held in Donegal Town on Wednesday 11 February. It was decided that the two Ballyshannon players would be suspended until 1 May, while the club ground was deemed unplayable until 1 March.[131] Donegal were awarded the match, and the *Donegal Independent* concluded their report by claiming that 'outside of the players there were not fifty males over the age of twelve years on the field, and of these two thirds were on the opposite side from the fracas'.[132] The newspaper also heavily criticised the referee and this brought an end to the coverage of the Britton Cup in the local press for 1914.[133] The tournament was won by Killybegs Emeralds and they went on to win it again in 1915, although this does not appear to have been recorded in the local press at the time.[134] With neighbouring rivalries and failure to comply with the rules, local soccer matches must have been extremely difficult to conduct, although it could be argued that an 'outside' referee would have been more appropriate.

NAME	AGE	OCCUPATION
Robert Quinn	23	Staff of family-run hotel
Frank P. Cunningham	Unknown	Shop Owner
Jack Sheridan	33	Shop Owner
Eddie Gallagher	33	Shop Assistant
John Heslin	Unknown	Teacher in Industrial School
Charlie Murrin	28	Staff in family-run shop
John James McGettigan	25	Butcher
Alfie Boyle	Unknown	Musician
Patrick Flynn	Unknown	Staff of Industrial School
Charlie McIntyre	34	Shop Assistant
Joe Murrin	22	Agent for meal and flour
Joe Cunningham	24	Building Contractor

Tony Conwell	31	Ran mail car
Frank O'Hara	27	Blacksmith
Willie Joe Molloy	25	Fishing Agent/Salesman
John Lavery	20	Boat Builder
Joe Ward	Unknown	Solicitor
Charlie Green	28	Assistant in family-run shop
Charles Eddie Cannon	20	Shop Assistant

Table 8: Killybegs Emeralds, 1914/15.

BRITTON CUP WINNING SQUAD AND OFFICIALS

This Killybegs Emeralds team partly consisted of those owning or employed in shops or businesses, not unlike the 1906 team. Others were skilled tradesmen and some had qualified from college. While this early foundation and growth in Killybegs would see soccer largely unchallenged in the town's number-one ball game until the emergence of their GAA club in the 1980s, other areas in Donegal which would go on to develop a strong tradition of Gaelic games did not manage to establish a GAA club like Ballyshannon had in 1909 until after the War of Independence. One of these was Kilcar, in the south-west of the county, and the playing of soccer in this area in the early years of the twentieth century has been well documented in the club's history, published in 1984.

The area's proximity to Killybegs was seen as an important factor in the playing of soccer, and again ships' teams, most notably the *Platypus* and the *Vulcan*, were seen as being conducive to developing an interest in the game there. It was also noted that the majority of the Kilcar players which took on the *Platypus* team in 1914 were attending college at the time and brought their sporting interests home with them. Michéal O'Domhnaill also states that a number of these would go on to play Gaelic football in the 1920s, as in Ardara, as the town became increasingly well known for its Gaelic football.[135]

DONEGAL GAA CLUBS 1913-14

At the end of 1913, the Aodh Ruadh hurling club held their fourth annual ball[136] and they would appear to have been the most consistently run GAA club in the county at this time, in spite of the poor state of the association

Killybegs Emeralds FC, Britton Cup Winners, 1914–15. (Courtesy of Moira Mallon)

there. They also held their AGM at the beginning of March 1914 in the Rock Hall, which was well attended, and it was revealed that they had a credit balance of £9 18*s* 10*d*. The club were keen to revive Gaelic football in the county and decided to begin football training immediately.[137]

Despite reports on matches being played in Letterkenny between the local Celtic team and Emmets of Derry at St Eunan's College that same month, little progress was being made with the sport in Donegal.[138] Calls from 'Shaun Ruadh' in the Derry GAA notes for GAA teams in Letterkenny, Ramelton and Buncrana to become more involved with their Derry neighbours[139] went ignored, and Aodh Ruadh's Gaelic football training does not appear to have been very fruitful that year.

In preparation for their annual sports that June, which was well organised with an enclosure and admission fee put in place at the Gaelic Park along with a brass band being asked to perform, the club had advertised a tug-of-war competition which was open to 'hurling and Gaelic football clubs and combatants of Irish Volunteers'.[140] It was estimated in the *Derry Journal* that by 29 May, there were 5,500 Irish National Volunteers enlisted in Donegal out of a nationwide total of 130,000.[141] Unfortunately it is difficult to establish just how many of these were involved in GAA clubs in the county. A team calling itself the Letterkenny 'Volunteers' played out a draw against Sarsfields of Derry in late August, but there is little else recorded about their activities.[142]

THE IRISH NATIONAL VOLUNTEERS

While nationally the GAA has been keen to promote an image of Irish Volunteer involvement in the organisation, Paul Rouse is highly dismissive of this notion. He feels that the association, despite having its prominent officials 'make sympathetic speeches and pass sympathetic motions', was more interested in its administrative duties at the time, and that GAA involvement in the Volunteers was 'minimal'.[143] Certainly in Donegal, the Inspector General of the RIC did not deem any GAA activity noteworthy in the first half of the year, and the small number of GAA clubs escaped mention in the list of organisations prominent in the county around this time.

There is also little evidence to suggest Volunteer activity in soccer clubs, although it was reported in the *Derry Journal* that on 3 September 1914, 'about 2,000 spectators assembled at Rathmullan' to see the home soccer club defeat Derry side Old Timers by 2–1.[144] A month later, plans for the Old Timers' team to travel to Letterkenny on 11 October were published. It was claimed that:

> … the Letterkenny Irish National Volunteers under Sergeant Major Corrigan's leadership will meet the visitors in the Cathedral town, and headed by the local fife and drum band will escort the Old Timers to their Hotel. After the football match, a review of the volunteers will take place in the field, and the band will discourse a number of selections.[145]

Reporting of this event was not continued and unsurprisingly, by September, the First World War was beginning to dominate the local press. Throughout the rest of 1914 there was little mention of sport in the *Derry Journal*. It is equally difficult to trace the number of GAA or soccer players who fought in the Great War, although one prominent Killybegs soccer player was not forgotten in the local press. He was Private Patrick Murrin of the Irish Guards, who was killed in battle on Easter Monday 1915 at Neuve Chapelle, leaving behind a young wife.[146] As previously mentioned, Sproule Myles was decorated and returned home. The topic of Donegal sportsmen who served in battle is surely worthy of future research.

THE REORGANISATION OF THE GAA IN DONEGAL IN 1919

Emigration, the Great War and the struggle for independence meant that local GAA competitions went further into decline in this decade. The Donegal GAA county board was not reorganised until April 1919,[147] and Donegal was the final Ulster county to be affiliated with the GAA at the Ulster Council AGM in Derry City that year.[148] It was not until the 1920s that GAA clubs began to be reformed in Donegal and the playing of Gaelic football and hurling championships became more frequent. In April 1922, the clubs of Castlefin, Glenties, Ardara, Bundoran, Donegal, Killybegs, Letterkenny and Ballyshannon were all represented at a GAA county board meeting held under the presidency of P.J. Ward, TD.[149]

This transformation from soccer to Gaelic games in some parishes is apparent in the number of clubs formed or reformed in the south and south-west of the county in this decade. Ardara (1921), Glenties (1921), Maghery (Dungloe) (1923), Kilcar (1924), and Donegal Young Tírconaills (1924) all had sufficient numbers to organise the playing of Gaelic games, and this illustrates the level of patriotic feeling in these areas after the War of Independence, as a number of clubs finally turned against the playing of soccer. Aodh Ruadh, who had also gone into decline despite their hurling progress, were able to reorganise in 1924, and found assistance from the local clergy, often a significant factor in the development of GAA clubs.[150]

This development was strengthened by the arrival of Garda Síochána from other counties who would take on a significant role in administration and playing, while national school teachers again began to put their spare time and money into the organisation. Given that most rural towns and villages would have had only a few people involved in organising sport, the switch to Gaelic games would have left little choice of sport for others in the area. Both groups would have had a structured working week with time to meet, and been at a suitable age for playing. The *Donegal Democrat*, founded in 1919, also began to raise the profile of the organisation in the county.

CONCLUSION

The enthusiasm shown towards the Gaelic Revival in 1905 and 1906 by those in Mountcharles and Donegal Town was not strong enough to maintain the Donegal GAA county board in 1907. The Gaelic League in County Donegal lacked the power to generate a widespread change in the attitudes shown by the general public towards soccer, and in Donegal Town the Balldeargs club did not get the support they felt they deserved to challenge the game as the number-one pastime in the locality.

It is clear that soccer was established in many towns throughout the county at this stage and the loss of Seumas MacManus and Richard Bonner meant that Gaelic games in south Donegal lacked the leaders needed to manipulate their growth and promote their continuation.

It is also clear that the clergy of the Catholic Church lessened their support for the movement and Bishop O'Donnell's involvement with the Irish Parliamentary Party, and his desire to see Home Rule, meant that he was always going to maintain a healthy distance from the Sinn Féin party and MacManus, who advocated a more militaristic style of gaining power. Similarly, Canon McFadden and the Very Revd Dr Maguire seem to have eased off in their support of the GAA after 1906. The lack of communication between the two county boards did little to help the association's development, with the poor turnout reported at western board meetings linked to attendance difficulties for 'countryside' delegates. It is not clear how much funding they received from would-be patrons or the Ulster GAA Council around this time.

Soccer was firmly established in Inishowen and the north-east of Donegal and would have been easier to organise, with a clearer understanding of the rules and clubs being in place there since the early 1890s. Despite attempts to re-establish Gaelic games in 1911, there simply wasn't enough support or GAA clubs in the county, and soccer clubs such as Killybegs Emeralds were growing in strength. The problems encountered by the Woods Cup committee in Ballyshannon highlighted the lack of respect for organising bodies, which had been a problem since the 1890s. It must also be noted that the Aodh Ruadh GAA club in Ballyshannon, founded by the local Gaelic League in 1909, managed to compete with soccer in the area by promoting hurling, and they appear to have had a good relationship with the local soccer clubs, unlike that of the Balldearg club, and perhaps this was fundamental to their growth in the years immediately prior to 1914.

However, the small number of GAA clubs Donegal in these years illustrates that both Gaelic football and hurling were in their infancy there, and it was not until the years after the foundation of the Irish Free State that the GAA was able to gain a proper foothold in the county (although this was not the case in all areas, most notably in Inishowen and the north-east, which continued to maintain its soccer tradition).

EPILOGUE

It is clear that the social, political and economic climate in County Donegal in the late Victorian era was such that a number of the factors which were fundamental to the sporting revolution in Britain around that time could not exist. It was not until the early 1890s, during the era of Muscular Christianity, that the number of soccer clubs in Donegal began to grow, and in areas such as the north-east of the county the influence of those involved in soccer in Derry City was apparent.

At times, these clubs grew from other social gatherings and they were often founded by local businessmen for the benefit of the youth of their areas. The Donegal FA, which ran from 1894-98, was instigated by national school teacher Daniel Deeney, but lasted only briefly and was hampered by administrative problems. Its original clubs were all located near the Letterkenny area, with the exception of Derrybeg FC. These limitations with transport meant that teams from south Donegal did not become affiliated until the association's final season. Lack of funding was also a factor in its decline, but a number of these soccer clubs were now established and geographical boundaries were beginning to be set down.

GAA clubs in north Donegal also looked to Derry for leadership in the late 1880s/early 1890s, but only two of these survived to become part of the 1905 GAA county board which was established as part of the Gaelic revival. Their competitions were developed partly in reaction to the planned organisation of the Evans soccer cup in Ardara. Seumas MacManus's aims that the youth of the county would become more involved in the GAA and that Gaelic games would become firmly established did not ultimately receive enough support, either from would-be patrons or indeed prospective players who were more interested in playing soccer in many areas and did not feel it necessary for this to cease. The two GAA boards were not working together, and by 1907 the organisation was coming to a close. However, 1905–6 had seen the first serious challenge to the playing of soccer in County Donegal.

In Ballyshannon, military involvement was fundamental to the development of soccer in 1896, and by 1905, local club Erne FC was able to challenge opposition from outside the county. The first Woods soccer cup took place in the town in 1909 and the Gaelic League were instrumental in founding a GAA club there around the same time. A number of soccer clubs such as Ardara Emeralds and Killybegs Emeralds drew their players from those in the eighteen to thirty-five age group who had some free time on their hands and flexible working hours (many were shop assistants and salesmen).

The social and economic conditions prevalent in Donegal at the time did little to help the development of soccer and Gaelic games in this period, and it is evident that a proper structure for competitions in Gaelic games in Donegal was not firmly established until the mid-1920s. During this time, public opinion began to turn against the British, with the events of the War of Independence, and many began to see soccer as a British sport (most notably in the west, south and south-west of the county). This is evident in the number of GAA clubs which were formed in these areas around this time, and also in the re-emergence of the county board and county championships. Soccer continued to retain its popularity over Gaelic games in the north and east of the county and this pattern has continued to the present day.

Improved communications and the development of the transport network in the county meant that the organisation of these pastimes became more effective and as a result became a more accessible social outlet for the people of Donegal than it had been in the years 1881–1914.

ENDNOTES

INTRODUCTION

[1] Neal Garnham, *Association Football and Society in Pre-partition Ireland* (Belfast: Ulster Historical Foundation, 2004), p.7.

[2] *Ibid.* p.8.

[3] Mike Cronin, *Sport and Nationalism in Ireland – Gaelic Games, Soccer and Irish Identity since 1884* (Dublin: Four Courts Press, 1999), p.103.

[4] *Ibid.*, p.104.

[5] *Ibid.*

[6] *Ibid.*, pp107–9.

[7] Tom Garvin, *The Evolution of Irish Nationalist Politics* (Dublin: Gill & Macmillan, 2005), p.111.

[8] *Derry Journal* (hereafter referred to as *DJ*), 12 February 1906.

[9] W.F. Mandle, 'Sport as politics: the Gaelic Athletic Association 1884-1916' in Cashman & McKernan (eds) *Sport in History* (Brisbane: Queensland University Press, 1979), pp99–123, pp100–1.

[10] *Ibid.* p.100.

[11] Garnham, *Association Football*, p.30.

[12] *DJ*, 31 October 1927.

[13] Garnham, *Association Football*, p.14.

[14] Jim MacLaughlin, 'The politics of nation-building in post-famine Donegal' in Nolan, Ronayne & Dunlevy (eds) *Donegal History and Society. Inter-disciplinary Essays on the History of an Irish County* (Dublin: Geography Publications, 1995), pp583–621, p.587.

[15] Campbell, Dowds & Mullan, *Against the Grain. A history of Burt, its people and the GAA.* (Burt, 2000), p.142.

[16] Paul Rouse, 'Sport and Ireland in 1881' in Alan Bairner, *Sport and the Irish – histories, identities, issues* (Dublin: University College Dublin Press, 2005), pp7–21, p.16.

[17] *Ibid.*

[18] Sean MacConaill (ed.), *Idir peil agus pobal. A History of the GAA in the parish of Ardara 1921-2003* (Ardara: Black Lion Books, 2004).

[19] Micheal O'Domhnaill (ed.), *CLG Cill Chartha 1924-1984* (Donegal: CLG Cill Chartha, 1984).

[20] Campbell, Dowds & Mullan.

[21] Eamonn Monaghan, *Remembering our founders* (Mountcharles: CLG Dun na nGall, 1997).

CHAPTER ONE

[1] MacLaughlin, p.587.
[2] *Ibid.*, p.611.
[3] *Ibid.*, p.587.
[4] *Ibid.*, pp587-8
[5] Pat Bolger, 'The congested districts board and the co-ops in Donegal' in Nolan, Ronayne & Dunlevy, pp 649-71, p.649.
[6] *DJ*, 26 August 1891.
[7] *Ibid.*, 8 May 1891.
[8] *Ibid.*, 26 August 1891.
[9] *Ibid.*, 2 September 1865.
[10] *Ibid.*, 24 July 1876.
[11] Bolger, p.649.
[12] *Ibid.*, p.650.
[13] *Ibid.*
[14] *Ibid.*
[15] Neil Tranter, *Sport, Economy and Society in Britain, 1750-1914* (Cambridge: Cambridge University Press, 1998), p.29.
[16] Jim MacLaughlin, 'Donegal and the New Ireland – The age of transition' in *Donegal – The Making of a Northern County* (Dublin: Four Courts Press, 2007), pp 283-357, p.284.
[17] Rouse, 'Sport and Ireland in 1881', p.8.
[18] *Ibid.*
[19] *Ibid.*, p.9.
[20] H. Meehan & G. Duffy, *Tracing your Donegal Ancestors* (Dublin: Flyleaf Press, 2008), p.100.
[21] Pádraig Ó Baoighill, *Cardinal Patrick O'Donnell 1856-1927* (Fintown: Chró na mBothán, 2008), p.180.
[22] *Ibid.*, p.181.
[23] Tranter, *Sport, economy and society in Britain 1750-1914*. p.26.
[24] *Ibid.*
[25] Matthew Taylor, *The Association Game – A History of British Football* (Harlow: Pearson Education Limited, 2008), p.38.
[26] *Ibid.*
[27] *DJ*, 18 December 1897.
[28] Graham McColl, *Hamlyn Illustrated History – Celtic, 1888-1998* (London: Hamlyn, 1998), p.10.
[29] Email from Chris Cameron, 12 August 2008.
[30] Willie Maley, *The Story of the Celtic* (Glasgow: Villafield Press, 1939), p.3.
[31] Henry Boylan, *A Dictionary of Irish Biography* (Dublin: Gill & Macmillan, 1978), p.81.
[32] Bernard O'Hara, 'Michael Davitt remembered' in Sean Beattie (ed.) *The Donegal Annual 2007 – Journal of the County Donegal Historical Society* (Letterkenny: Browne Printers Ltd, 2007), pp213-8, p.213.
[33] Maley, p.15.
[34] *Ibid.*, p.2.
[35] *Ibid.*, pp3-4.
[36] Cameron Email, 12 August 2008.
[37] *DJ*, Friday 27 September 1895.
[38] Ben O'Donnell, *The story of the Rosses* (Letterkenny: Browne Printers, 1999), p.381.
[39] Derek Doherty, *The History of the GAA in Donegal* Unpublished MA thesis (Maynooth, 1998), p.27.
[40] O'Donnell, *The story of the Rosses*, p.382.
[41] Frank Sweeney, *The Murder of Connell Boyle, County Donegal, 1898* (Dublin: Four Courts Press, 2002), p.57.
[42] Pat Conaghan, *The Zulu Fishermen. Forgotten Pioneers of Donegal's First Fishing Industry* (Killybegs: Bygones Enterprise, 2003), p.35.

[43] *Thom's Irish almanac and official directory of the United Kingdom of Great Britain and Ireland for the year 1897* (London: Alexander Thom, 1897), p.1,061.

[44] http://www.inishowennews.com/08GreenMemorable.htm 24 September 2009.

[45] Mike Huggins, 'The spread of Association football in North-east England, 1876-90: the pattern of diffusion' in *The International Journal of the History of Sport,* vol.6, no.3, December 1989 (London: Frank Cass, 1989), pp299-318, p.300.

[46] *DJ*, 24 September 1884.

[47] Pádraig S. Mac a' Ghoill, '100 years of the GAA in Donegal' in the *Donegal Annual 1984, no.36* (Ballyshannon: Donegal Democrat Printing, 1984), pp 89-94, p.89.

[48] *DJ*, 4 October 1886.

[49] *Ibid.*, 8 October 1886.

[50] *Thom's Irish almanac and official directory of the United Kingdom of Great Britain and Ireland for the year 1884* (London: Alexander Thom, 1884), p.1,057.

[51] *Ibid.*

[52] Steve Flanders, *The County Donegal Railway – A visitor's guide* (Leicester: Midland Publishing, 1996), p.4.

[53] *Ibid.*

[54] Alvin Jackson, *Ireland 1798-1998* (Oxford: Blackwell Publishing Ltd, 1999), p.181.

[55] *Ibid.*, pp181-82.

[56] Cronin, *Sport and Nationalism in Ireland*, p.76.

[57] *Ibid.*

[58] John Tunney, 'The marquis, the reverend, the grandmaster and the major: Protestant politics in Donegal, 1868-1933' in Nolan, Ronayne & Dunlevy, pp675-94, p.675.

[59] *Ibid.*

[60] *Ibid.*, p.677.

[61] *Ibid.*, p.678.

[62] *Ibid.*, p.683.

[63] *Ibid.*, p.684.

[64] Campbell, Dowds & Mullan, p.70.

[65] Eoin Kinsella, 'Riotous proceedings and the cricket of savages: football and hurling in early modern Ireland' in Cronin, Murphy & Rouse (eds), *The Gaelic Athletic Association, 1884-2009* (Dublin: Irish Academic Press, 2009), pp15-31, p.19.

[66] Liam P. Ó Caithnia, *Scéal na hIomana* (Baile Atha Cliath: An Clochomhar Tta, 1980).

[67] P.S. Mac a' Ghoill, 'Cross-country hurling in Ardara' in *CLCG Ard a ratha* (Ardara: CLG Ard a Ratha, 1980), pp53-7, p.55.

[68] Cronin, *Sport and Nationalism*, p.74-5.

[69] *Ibid.*

[70] *Ibid.*, p.75

[71] *Ibid.*

[72] Neal Garnham (ed.), *The Origins and Development of Sport in Ireland:Being a Reprint of R.M. Peter's Irish Football Annual of 1880* (Belfast: Ulster Historical Foundation, 1999), p.10.

[73] *Ibid.*, p.20.

[74] *Ibid.*

[75] *DJ*, 14 March 1906.

[76] *Ibid.*, 19 March 1906.

[77] W.F. Mandle, 'The Gaelic Athletic Association and popular culture' in MacDonagh, Mandle & Pauric Travers (eds), *Irish Culture and Nationalism 1750-1950* (London: Macmillan in association with the Humanities Research Centre, Australian National University, 1983), p.111.

[78] *Ibid.*, p.112.

[79] *Ibid.*

[80] *Ibid.*

[81] These books contain a number of references to the playing of camán in their respective areas.
[82] Ó Caithnia, p.644.
[83] Seán Ó Heochaidh, Creideann in Inis Bó Finne, MS917, Folklore Commission 1943, pp48–52.
[84] Seán Ó Heochaidh, Christmas Day traditions in Cloughaneely, MS932, Folklore Commission 1943, pp455–462.
[85] Seamus King, *A History of Hurling* (Dublin: Gill & Macmillan, 1996), p.219.
[86] *Ibid.*
[87] *Ibid.*, p.220.
[88] Mac a' Ghoill, '100 Years of the GAA in Donegal', p.89.
[89] *Ibid.*
[90] King, p.221.
[91] *Ibid.*
[92] Mac a' Ghoill, 'Cross-country hurling in Ardara', p.53.
[93] Census of Ireland 1901. Donegal. DED Glengesh, 40/1 Aighe; 40/3 Brackey; 40/28 Scadaman; 40/31 Glengesh.
[94] Campbell, Dowds & Mullan, pp80–81.
[95] *DJ*, 18 July 1906.
[96] *Ibid.*, 15 July 1907.
[97] Campbell, Dowds & Mullan, p.xiii.
[98] MacConaill, p.8.
[99] 'Donegal GAA Club Map-Map of Donegal and its clubs' (http://gaainfo.com/countymap.php?co=donegal) 23 June 2009.
[100] *DJ*, 16 April 1886.
[101] *Ibid.*
[102] *Ibid.*, 24 December 1886.
[103] *Ibid.*, 29 December 1886.
[104] *Ibid.*
[105] *Ibid.*
[106] *The Sport*, 23 June 1888.
[107] Campbell, Dowds & Mullan, p.74.
[108] *Ibid.*, p.77.
[109] *The Sport*, 23 June 1888.
[110] *Ibid.*, 17 November 1888.
[111] *DJ*, 19 November 1888.
[112] Boylan, p.258.
[113] *DJ*, 24 December 1888.
[114] *Ibid.*, 28 January 1889.
[115] *Ibid.*, 1 April 1889.
[116] *Ibid.*
[117] *Ibid.*, 30 October 1889.
[118] *Ibid.*, 7 August 1889.
[119] *Ibid.*, 22 November 1889.
[120] *Ibid.*, 30 December 1889.
[121] *Ibid.*
[122] *Ibid.*, 31 January 1890.
[123] *Ibid*, 21 April 1890.
[124] *Ibid.*, 24 September 1890.
[125] *Ibid.*, 3 October 1890.
[126] *The Sport*, 6 December 1890.
[127] *DJ*, 16 March 1891.
[128] *Ibid.*, 27 March 1891.

[129] *DJ*, 29 April 1892.
[130] Campbell, Dowds & Mullan, p.80.
[131] Con Short, *The Ulster GAA Story* (Rossan: the Ulster GAA Committee, 1984), p.31.
[132] *DJ*, 12 August 1892.
[133] *Ibid.*, 17 August 1892.
[134] *Ibid.*, 30 December 1892.
[135] Campbell, Dowds & Mullan, p.80.
[136] *DJ*, 2 January 1893.
[137] Seán Ó Casaide, 'It was the Gaelic Leaguers who rallied Donegal' in *Irish Press GAA Supplement* (1934), p.40.
[138] *Crime Branch (Special). Precis of Reports and Suggestions.* The Chief Secretary's Office, Dublin Castle, 1891, CO904/16.279.
[139] *Crime Branch. Gaelic Athletic Association. Comparative Statement showing number of branches by counties in 1889, and at the end of the past year.* The Chief Secretary's Office, Dublin Castle, 1891, CO904/16 281/1.
[140] Garvin, p.97.
[141] Mac a' Ghoill, '100 years of the GAA in Donegal', p.89.
[142] Mandle, 'The Gaelic Athletic Association and popular culture, 1884-1924', p.107.
[143] Campbell, Dowds & Mullan, p.80.
[144] *Ibid.*
[145] *Donegal Independent* (hereafter referred to as *DI*), 20 April 1889.
[146] *Ibid.*
[147] *Donegal Vindicator* (hereafter referred to as *DV*), 4 January 1890.

CHAPTER TWO

[1] *DJ*, 25 April 1894.
[2] Garnham, *Association Football and Society in Pre-partition Ireland*, pp4-5.
[3] J. Sugden and A. Bairner, *Sport, Sectarianism and Society in a Divided Ireland* (Leicester: Leicester University Press, 1993), p.71.
[4] Cronin, *Sport and Nationalism in Ireland*, p.119.
[5] Eoghan Corry, *Going to America – World Cup 1994* (Dublin: Poolbeg, 1994), p.84.
[6] *DJ*, 25 July 1881.
[7] *Ibid.*
[8] *Ibid.*, 30 January 1882.
[9] *Ibid.*, 9 August 1882.
[10] *Ibid.*
[11] *Ibid.*
[12] *Ibid.*, 1 February 1882.
[13] *Ibid.*
[14] *Ibid.*, 24 April 1882.
[15] *Ibid.*, 13 October 1882.
[16] *Ibid.*
[17] *DJ*, 23 February 1885.
[18] *Ibid.*
[19] *Ibid.*, 12 June 1885.
[20] Neil Tranter, *Sport, Economy and Society in Britain 1750-1914*, p.56.
[21] *DJ*, 23 July 1886.
[22] *Ibid.*, April 7 1890.
[23] Garnham, *Association Football and Society in Pre-partition Ireland*, p.5.
[24] In 1891 the *Donegal Vindicator* and *Derry Journal* contained a number of references to these clubs.

[25] *DI*, 26 April 1890.
[26] *DV*, 1 May 1891.
[27] *DJ*, 5 February 1892.
[28] *Ibid.*, 21 March 1892.
[29] *Ibid.*
[30] *Ibid.*
[31] *Ibid.*, 21 October 1891.
[32] *Ibid.*, 28 October 1891.
[33] *Ibid.*
[34] *Ibid.*, 28 April 1893.
[35] In 1893, teams representing Dunkineely Wanderers, Inver Swifts, Milford Swifts, Carradoan FC(Rathmullan), Lifford, St Adaman's Swifts (Letterkenny), Bundoran Swifts, Finner Rakes, Mountcharles Gaels, Meenagram Celts, Kincasslagh, Gweedore Hearts, Tirlaghan, Cranford, Castlefin FC, Castlefin Bright Stars, Ramelton FC, Ramelton Sunbursts, Bundoran FC, Ballybofey, Boylagh Champions (Kilclooney), Young Bloods (Narin), Moville, Greencastle, Kerrykeel FC, Letterkenny FC, Meenacross, Meenacross Swifts, Burtonport, and Ards FC were all noted in the *Derry Journal*, *Donegal Independent* or *Donegal Vindicator* newspapers.
[36] On 23 September 1891, the *Derry Journal* reported that Milford Swifts defeated Letterekenny by 1-9 to 1-4 in an eleven-aside match in Milford. The game was well attended and Milford wore their new green kits with a white cross on the chest, supplied by Messrs Chase & Co., Letterkenny. Both teams had one umpire, and two linesmen were involved in this match, which lasted for an hour.
[37] The *Donegal Vindicator* reported on a match between the Joys and Green Volunteers at Letterkenny which ended 1-3 to 0-6 in November 1891.
[38] *DJ*, 4 September 1893.
[39] *Ibid.*
[40] *DJ*, 3 October 1894.
[41] *Ibid.*, 29 October 1894.
[42] *DJ*, 9 March 1894.
[43] *Ibid.*, 12 February 1894.
[44] *Ibid.*, 26 February 1894.
[45] *Ibid.*, 21 March 1894.
[46] *Ibid.*, 9 March 1894.
[47] *Ibid.*
[48] *Ibid.*
[49] *DV*, 14 October 1892.
[50] *Ibid.*, 18 November 1892.
[51] *DJ*, 16 March 1894.
[52] *DV*, 30 March 1894.
[53] *DJ*, 16 March 1894.
[54] *Ibid.*, 28 March 1894.
[55] *Ibid.*, 30 March 1894.
[56] *Ibid.*
[57] *Ibid.*, 25 April 1894.
[58] *Ibid.*
[59] *Ibid.*, 2 March 1894.
[60] *Ibid.*
[61] *Ibid.*
[62] *Ibid.*, 19 September 1894.
[63] *The Sport*, 22 September 1894.
[64] *DJ*, 7 November 1894.

[65] Neal Garnham, 'Football and identity in pre-Great War Ireland' in *Irish Economic and Social History*, no.*28* (Dublin: Economic and Social History Society of Ireland, 2001), pp13-31, p.16.
[66] *Ibid.*
[67] *DJ*, 12 December 1894.
[68] *Ibid.*
[69] *Ibid.*, 17 December 1894.
[70] *Ibid.*
[71] *Ibid.*
[72] *Ibid.*, 31 December 1894.
[73] *DV*, 7 September 1894.
[74] *DJ*, 10 September 1897.
[75] *Ibid.*, 22 September 1893.
[76] *Ibid.*, 27 February 1895.
[77] *Ibid.*, 24 April 1895.
[78] *Ibid.*, 25 March 1895.
[79] *Ibid.*, 1 April 1895.
[80] *Ibid.*, 25 March 1895.
[81] *Ibid.*, 8 April 1895.
[82] *DI*, 21 June 1895.
[83] *DJ*, 24 May 1895.
[84] *Ibid.*
[85] *Ibid.*, 31 May 1895.
[86] *Ibid.*
[87] *Ibid.*, 27 September 1895.
[88] *Ibid.*, 13 November 1895.
[89] *Ibid.*, 22 November 1895.
[90] *Ibid.*, 8 January 1896.
[91] *Ibid.*, 4 March 1896.
[92] *Ibid.*
[93] *Ibid.*, 6 March 1896.
[94] *Ibid.*
[95] *Ibid.*
[96] *Ibid.*, 3 June 1896.
[97] *Ibid.*
[98] Alan Metcalfe, 'Football in the mining communities of East Northumberland, 1882-1914' in *The International Journal of the History of Sport*, vol.5, no.3, December 1988 (London: Frank Cass, 1988), pp269-291, p.278.
[99] *DJ*, 3 June 1896.
[100] *Ibid.*
[101] *Ibid.*, 5 October 1896.
[102] *Ibid.*, 24 February 1897.
[103] *Ibid.*, 16 April 1897.
[104] *Ibid.*, 28 May 1897.
[105] *Ibid.*, 10 September 1897.
[106] *DJ*, 8 Feb 1888.
[107] *Ibid.*
[108] Campbell, Dowds & Mullan, p.74.
[109] *DJ*, 28 Dec 1888.
[110] *Ibid.*, 1 April 1898.
[111] *Ibid.*, 15 April 1898.
[112] *Ibid.*, 31 March 1909.

[113] *Ibid.*, 2 March 1898.
[114] Garnham, *Association Football and Society in Pre-partition Ireland*, p.21.
[115] *DV*, 23 February 1889.
[116] *Ibid.*, 27 April 1889.
[117] *Ibid.*, 2 November 1889.
[118] *Ibid.*, 17 April 1891.
[119] *Ibid.*
[120] *Ibid.*
[121] *Ibid.*, 19 February 1897.
[122] *Ibid.*, 18 September 1896.
[123] *DI*, 28 February 1896.
[124] *Ibid.*, 13 March 1896.
[125] *Ibid.*
[126] *Ibid.*
[127] *DV*, 13 March 1896.
[128] *DI*, 20 March 1896.
[129] *DV*, 3 April 1896.
[130] *Ibid.*
[131] *Ibid.*
[132] *DI*, 3 April 1896.
[133] *DV*, 24 April 1896.
[134] *Ibid.*, 8 May 1896.
[135] *Ibid.*, 28 August 1896.
[136] *Ibid.*, 18 September 1896.
[137] *Ibid.*
[138] *Ibid.*, 21 March 1902.
[139] *DJ*, 25 November 1896.
[140] John B. Cunningham, 'The port of Ballyshannon' in *the Donegal Annual 2000, no.52* (Letterkenny: Browne Printers Ltd, 2000), pp7–37.
[141] *Donegal Democrat* (hereafter referred to as *DD*), 17 February 1956.
[142] *Ibid.*
[143] *DJ*, 16 March 1898.
[144] *Ibid.*
[145] *DV*, 4 November 1898.
[146] *Ibid.*, 2 December 1898.
[147] *Ibid.*, 4 November 1898.
[148] *DI*, 30 December 1898.
[149] *DV*, 30 December 1898.
[150] *Ibid.*, 3 February 1899.
[151] *Ibid.*, 10 February 1899.
[152] *Ibid.*, 17 February 1899.
[153] *Ibid.*, 29 November 1901.
[154] *Ibid.*, 7 May 1897.
[155] *Ibid.*, 14 January 1898.
[156] *DJ*, 30 November 1898.
[157] *DV*, 14 February 1902.
[158] *Ibid.*, 5 June 1903.
[159] *Ibid.*
[160] *DJ*, 19 February 1904.
[161] *Ibid.*, 4 November 1904.
[162] Metcalfe, p.279.

CHAPTER THREE

[1] *DJ*, 1 March 1905.
[2] *Ibid.*, 20 January 1905.
[3] *Ibid.*, 18 December 1907.
[4] *Ibid.*, 30 January 1905.
[5] *Ibid.*
[6] Seosamh Ó Ceallaigh (ed.), *Aspects of our rich inheritance (Cloughaneely)* (Falcarragh: Dulra, 2000), pp161–2.
[7] *DJ*, 30 January 1905.
[8] *Ibid.*, 5 April 1905.
[9] Harry Spence, 'The graveyard at St Conal's church' in *Dearcadh – The Ardara View, Christmas 1992* (Letterkenny: Donegal Stationery & Printing Co., 1992), p.41.
[10] *DJ*, 7 April 1899.
[11] *Ibid.*, 18 August 1902.
[12] Huggins, pp299–318.
[13] *DV*, 1 May 1891.
[14] *Ibid.*, 4 September 1891.
[15] *Ibid.*
[16] *Ibid.*
[17] *Ibid.*, 22 January 1892.
[18] *DI*, 17 May 1901.
[19] Helen Meehan, *Inver Parish in History* (Donegal, 2005), pp418–21.
[20] *DV*, 29 October 1897.
[21] Jackson, p.178.
[22] Meehan, *Inver Parish in History*, p.7.
[23] *Ibid.*
[24] Hunt, 'The GAA: A social structure and associated clubs' in Cronin, Murphy & Rouse, pp200–1.
[25] David Hassan, 'The GAA in Ulster' in Cronin, Murphy & Rouse, p.81.
[26] *Ibid.*
[27] *DV*, 22 April 1904.
[28] *Ibid.*, 13 May 1904.
[29] *Ibid.*, 27 October 1905.
[30] Timothy G. McMahon, *Grand opportunity – the Gaelic revival and Irish society* (New York, 2008), pp89–90.
[31] *DJ*, 1 March 1905.
[32] *Ibid.*, 17 February 1905.
[33] Cronin, *Sport and Nationalism in Ireland*, p.84.
[34] *Ibid.*, p.85.
[35] *DJ*, 21 April 1905.
[36] *Ibid.*, 15 Sept. 1905.
[37] *Ibid.*, 10 November 1905.
[38] *DI*, 4 May 1906.
[39] 'St Catherine's FC Profile' in the *Donegal Post*, 5 March 2008.
[40] Moira Mallon, 'Killybegs Emeralds' in *Dearcadh – the Ardara view 1996-7* (Letterkenny: Donegal Stationery & Printing Co., 1996), pp52–3.
[41] *Ibid.*
[42] *Ibid.*
[43] *Ibid.*
[44] Jackson, p.186.
[45] Diarmaid Ferriter, *The Transformation of Ireland 1900-2000* (London: Profile Books, 2004), p.81.
[46] Meehan, *Inver Parish in History*, p.239.

[47] *DJ*, 7 April 1905.
[48] *Ibid.*, 14 April 1905.
[49] *Ibid.*, 19 April 1905.
[50] *Ibid.*
[51] *Ibid.*, 7 June 1905.
[52] Garnham, *Football and National Identity in pre-Great War Ireland*, pp 18–19.
[53] *DJ*, 17 July 1905.
[54] *Ibid.*, 11 August 1905.
[55] *Ibid.*, 8 September 1905.
[56] *The Sport*, 16 September 1905.
[57] *Ibid.*
[58] *Ibid.*
[59] *Ibid.*, 2 October 1905.
[60] *DI*, 6 October 1905.
[61] *DJ*, 4 October 1905.
[62] *Ibid.*, 9 October 1905.
[63] *Ibid.*
[64] *Ibid.*
[65] *Ibid.*
[66] *Ibid.*
[67] Hunt, *Sport and Society in Victorian Ireland – The Case of Westmeath*, p.204.
[68] *Ibid.*
[69] Ó Casaide, p.40.
[70] *DJ*, 25 October 1905.
[71] *DJ*, 17 November 1905.
[72] *Ibid.*, 24 November 1905.
[73] *Ibid.*, 17 November 1905.
[74] *Ibid.*, 24 November 1905.
[75] *Ibid.*, 25 October 1905.
[76] *Ibid.*, 15 November 1905.
[77] *Ibid.*, 27 October 1905
[78] *Ibid.*
[79] Monaghan, p.9.
[80] Ferriter, p.36
[81] *DV*, 27 October 1905.
[82] *Ibid.*, 29 September 1905.
[83] *Ibid.*, 6 October 1905.
[84] *DD*, 4 November 1933
[85] *DJ*, 17 November 1905.
[86] *Ibid.*
[87] *Ibid.*, 24 November 1905.
[88] *Ibid.*, 29 December 1905.
[89] *Ibid.*, 11 July 1906.
[90] *Ibid.*, 20 September 1905.
[91] *Ibid.*
[92] *Ibid.*, 12 January 1906.
[93] *Ibid.*
[94] *Ibid.*, 6 April 1906.
[95] *Ibid.*, 18 May 1906.
[96] *Ibid.*
[97] *Ibid.*, 11 May 1906.

[98] *DI*, 4 May 1906.
[99] *Ibid.*, 1 June 1906.
[100] Hunt, *Sport and society in Victorian Ireland*, pp202–3.
[102] *DI*, 6 April 1906.
[103] *Ibid.*, 18 May 1906.
[104] *DI*, 9 March 1906.
[105] *DJ*, 22 January 1906.
[106] *Ibid.*, 9 May 1906.
[107] *DI*, 2 March 1906.
[108] *DV*, 7 December 1907.
[109] *Ibid.*, 26 July 1907.
[110] *DJ*, 26 January 1906.
[111] *DI*, 15 February 1907.
[112] *DJ*, 22 January 1906.
[113] *DI*, 13 July 1906.
[114] *DJ*, 27 April 1906.
[115] *Ibid.*, 18 April 1906.
[116] *Ibid.*, 4 April 1906.
[117] *Ibid.*
[118] *DI*, 4 May 1906.
[119] *DJ*, 3 June 1896. The poor conduct of spectators was highlighted as being a cause for concern at the association's AGM on 31 May 1896.
[120] *Ibid.*, 18 July 1906.
[121] Ó Casaide, p.40.
[122] *DJ*, 18 July 1906.
[123] *DI*, 26 October 1906 and 21 December 1906.
[124] *DJ*, 26 April 1907.
[125] *DI*, 13 July 1906.
[126] *DJ*, 18 July 1906.
[127] *Ibid.*
[128] *Ibid.*, 23 February 1906.
[129] *Ibid.*, 7 March 1906.
[130] *DI*, 4 May 1906.
[131] *Ibid.*
[132] *DJ*, 20 April 1906.
[133] *Ibid.*
[134] *Ibid.*, 16 January 1907.
[135] *Ibid.*, 26 June 1907.
[136] *Ibid.*, 27 January 1908.
[137] *Ibid.*, 26 February 1908.
[138] *Ibid.*, 15 May 1908.
[139] *Ibid.*, 11 February 1907.
[140] *Ibid.*, 15 June 1908.
[141] *DI*, 15 November 1901.

CHAPTER FOUR

[1] *DJ*, 2 August 1907
[2] *DI*, 19 October 1906.
[3] *Ibid.*
[4] *Ibid.*

[5] *DJ*, 28 November 1906.
[6] *Ibid.*, 11 January 1907.
[7] *Ibid.*, 2 August 1907.
[8] Campbell, Dowds & Mullan, p.140.
[9] *DI*, 1 February 1907.
[10] *Ibid.*, 26 April 1907.
[11] Ó Baoighill, p.259.
[12] *Ibid.*, pp284–5.
[13] *Ibid.*, p.259.
[14] *DJ*, 18 July 1906.
[15] Campbell, Dowds & Mullan, p.93.
[16] *DJ*, 9 September 1907.
[17] *Ibid.*
[18] *Ibid.*, 15 July 1907.
[19] Meehan, *Inver Parish in History*, p.427.
[20] Cahir Healy in *The Gaelic Athlete Annual and county directory for 1907-8* (Dublin, 1907), p.33.
[21] Helen Meehan, 'The MacManus brothers' in *The Donegal Annual 1994, no.46.* (Ballyshannon: Donegal Democrat Ltd, 1994), p.13.
[22] *DV*, 21 December 1906.
[23] Meehan, 'The MacManus brothers', p.15.
[24] *DJ*, 20 November 1908.
[25] *DJ*, 13 March 1911.
[26] *DI*, 30 December 1904.
[27] *Ibid.*, 28 November 1902.
[28] *DJ*, 18 December 1908.
[29] *Ibid.*, 15 September 1909.
[30] *DI*, 23 February 1906.
[31] *Ibid.*, 26 October 1906.
[32] *Ibid.*
[33] *DV*, 8 November 1907.
[34] *Ibid.*, 8 February 1907.
[35] *Ibid.*
[36] *Ibid.*, 15 March 1907.
[37] *DJ*, 26 July 1907.
[38] *RIC Crime Branch Special Department Report in D.M.P. District*, CO 904/11.1934S/375, 4 May 1908.
[39] *DI*, 31 July 1908.
[40] *Ibid.*, 7 August 1908.
[41] *Ibid.*
[42] Hunt, *Sport and Society in Victorian Ireland*, p.194.
[43] *DI*, 9 October 1908.
[44] *DJ*, 16 November 1908.
[45] *Ibid.*, 9 December 1908.
[46] *Ibid.*
[47] *Ibid.*
[48] *Ibid.*
[49] *The Sport*, 26 January 1907
[50] *Ibid.*, 23 June 1906.
[51] *DJ*, 31 March 1909.
[52] *Ibid.*, 21 April 1909.
[53] *Ibid.*, 5 July 1909.
[54] *Ibid.*

[55] *Ibid.*
[56] Garnham, *Association Football and Society in Pre-partition Ireland*, p.46.
[57] Ferriter, p.57.
[58] *DJ*, 5 February 1909.
[59] *Ibid.*, 27 June 1910.
[60] *Ibid.*, 13 July 1910.
[61] *Ibid.*, 12 August 1910.
[62] *DV*, 8 April 1904.
[63] *Ibid.*, 13 May 1904.
[64] *Ibid.*, 27 October 1905.
[65] *Ibid.*
[66] *Ibid.*, 29 September 1905.
[67] *Ibid.*, 3 November 1905.
[68] *Ibid.*
[69] Garnham, *Association Football and Society in Pre-partition Ireland*, p.23.
[70] *DV*, 27 October 1905.
[71] *Ibid.*, 13 October 1905.
[72] *Ibid.*, 17 November 1905.
[73] *Ibid.*
[74] *Ibid.*
[75] *Ibid.*
[76] *Ibid.*
[77] *Ibid.*, 27 November 1905.
[78] *Ibid.*, 1 December 1905.
[79] *The Sport*, 15 September 1906.
[80] *DI*, 7 December 1906.
[81] *DJ*, 29 October 1909.
[82] *DI*, 15 October 1909.
[83] *Ibid.*, 14 October 1910.
[84] *DJ*, 14 June 1911.
[85] *DI*, 10 June 1911.
[86] *Ibid.*, 14 October 1910.
[87] *Ibid.*, 4 March 1910.
[88] *Ibid.*, 7 July 1911.
[89] *Ibid.*, 4 August 1911.
[90] *DV*, 11 November 1911.
[91] *Ibid.*, 20 October 1910.
[92] *DI*, 16 February 1912.
[93] *Ibid.*, 15 November 1912.
[94] *DI*, 28 May 1897.
[95] *Ibid.*, 9 July 1897.
[96] *Ibid.*, 4 November 1904.
[97] *Ibid.*
[98] *DV*, 26 November 1909.
[99] *Ibid.*, 17 December 1909.
[100] *Ibid.*, 7 January 1910.
[101] *Ibid.*
[102] *Ibid.*
[103] *Ibid.*
[104] *Ibid.*, 30 September 1910
[105] *Ibid.*, 31 March 1911.

[106] *DJ*, 13 October 1911.
[107] *Ibid.*, 22 December 1911.
[108] Garnham, *Association Football and Society in Pre-partition Ireland*, p.101.
[109] *DJ*, 3 June 1896.
[110] *Ibid.*, 31 January 1912.
[111] Interview with Moira Mallon of Killybegs, County Donegal, 6 April 2009.
[112] *DV*, 5 April 1912.
[113] *DJ*, 17 April 1912.
[114] *Ibid.*
[115] *Ibid.*
[116] *DI*, 25 October 1912.
[117] *Ibid.*, 17 January 1913.
[118] *Ibid.*, 21 February 1913.
[119] *Ibid.*, 28 March 1913.
[120] *Ibid.*
[121] *Ibid.*, 11 April 1913.
[122] *DV*, 7 March 1913.
[123] *DJ*, 19 December 1913.
[124] *Ibid.*
[125] *DI*, 14 February 1914.
[126] *Ibid.*
[127] *Ibid.*
[128] *Ibid.*
[129] *Ibid.*, 31 January 1914.
[130] *Ibid.*, 14 February 1914.
[131] *Ibid.*
[132] *Ibid.*
[133] *Ibid.*
[134] Mallon, p.52.
[135] Michéal O'Domhnaill (ed.), *CLG Cill Chartha 1924-1984*, p.8.
[136] *DV*, 2 January 1914.
[137] *Ibid.*, 13 March 1914.
[138] *DV*, 13 March 1914.
[139] *DJ*, 6 March 1914.
[140] *Ibid.*, 20 June 1914.
[141] *Ibid.*, 1 June 1914.
[142] *DI*, 29 August 1914.
[143] Paul Rouse, 'The politics of culture and sport in Ireland: A history of the GAA ban on foreign games 1884-1971. Part one: 1884-1921', in *The International Journal of the History of Sport*, vol.10, no.3 (London: Frank Cass, 1993), pp333-360.
[144] *DJ*, 7 September 1914.
[145] *Ibid.*, 7 October 1914.
[146] *DI*, 15 May 1915.
[147] *DJ*, 11 April 1919.
[148] Campbell, Dowds & Mullan, p.94.
[149] *DD*, 7 April 1922.
[150] *Ibid.*, 8 February 1924.

BIBLIOGRAPHY

PRIMARY SOURCES

MANUSCRIPTS

The British in Ireland. Part One: Anti-Government organisations, 1882-1921, CO904/16 (microfilm).

The British in Ireland. Part One: Secret societies, précis of information and reports relating to the D.M.P. District (March 1905-December 1908), CO904/11 (microfilm).

Census of Ireland 1901: Donegal, manuscript returns of 1901 and 1911 census, Ardara, Glengesh and Killybegs and manuscript returns of 1911, Ballyshannon and Donegal (microfilm).

Church of the Holy Family, Ardara, baptism records (January 1868-July 1904).

Church of Ireland, Ardara, register of marriages, parish of Iniskeel (1845-1951).

Folklore Commission, MS917, MS932 (1943).

Slater's Directory (1881, 1894).

Raphoe Diocesan Archives, Cardinal O'Donnell papers.

NEWSPAPERS

Derry Journal

Donegal Democrat

Donegal Independent

Donegal Vindicator

The Sport

SECONDARY SOURCES

BOOKS

Bairner, Alan (ed.), *Sport and the Irish – histories, identities, issues* (Dublin: University College Dublin Press, 2005).

Boylan, Henry, *A Dictionary of Irish Biography* (Dublin: Gill & Macmillan, 1978).

Campbell, D., Dowds, D. & Mullan, D., *Against the Grain: A history of Burt, its people and the GAA* (Burt: 2000).

Cashman, R. & McKernan, M. (eds), *Sport in History* (Brisbane: Queensland University Press, 1979).

Conaghan, Pat, *Bygones – New Horizons on the History of Killybegs* (Killybegs: Bygones Enterprise, 1989).

Conaghan, Pat, *The Zulu Fishermen: Forgotten Pioneers of Donegal's First Fishing Industry* (Killybegs: Bygones Enterprise, 2003).

Corry, Eoghan, *Going to America – World Cup 1994* (Dublin: Poolbeg, 1994).

Cronin, Mike, *Sport and Nationalism in Ireland: Gaelic Games, Soccer and Irish Identity since 1884* (Dublin: Four Courts Press, 1999).

Cronin, M., Murphy, W. & Rouse, P. (eds), *The Gaelic Athletic Association, 1884-2009* (Dublin: Irish Academic Press, 2009).

Cullen, Tom, *Beart de Réir ár mBriathair. A History of the GAA in Ulster* (Belfast: Comhairle Uladh, 2004).

De Burca, Marcus, *The GAA – A history* (Dublin: Cumann Luthchleas Gael, 1980).

Ferriter, Diarmaid, *The Transformation of Ireland 1900-2000* (London: Profile Books, 2004).

Garnham, Neal, *Association Football and Society in Pre-partition Ireland* (Belfast: Ulster Historical Foundation, 2004).

Garnham, Neal (ed.), *The Origins and Development of Sport in Ireland: Being a Reprint of R.M. Peter's Irish Football Annual of 1880* (Belfast: Ulster Historical Foundation, 1999).

Garvin, Tom, *The Evolution of Irish Nationalist Politics* (Dublin: Gill & Macmillan, 2005).

Holland, Pat, *100 years of Handball. Handball, Donegal and the World* (Ballybofey: Voice Books, 2004).

Holt, Richard, *Sport and the British – A Modern History* (Oxford: Clarendon Press, 1989).

Hunt, Tom, *Sport and Society in Victorian Ireland – The Case of Westmeath* (Cork: Cork University Press, 2007).

Jackson, Alvin, *Ireland 1798-1998* (Oxford: Blackwell Publishing, 1999).

King, Seamus, *A History of Hurling* (Dublin: Gill & Macmillan, 1996).

Mac Conaill, Sean (ed.), *Idir Peil agus Pobal. A History of the GAA in the parish of Ardara 1921-2003* (Ardara: Black Lion Books, 2004).

McColl, Graham, *Hamlyn Illustrated History – Celtic, 1888-1998* (London: Hamlyn, 1998).

Mac a' Ghoill, Padraig S., '100 years of the G.A.A in Donegal' in the *Donegal Annual 1984, Number 36* (Ballyshannon: Donegal Democrat Ltd, 1984).

MacDonagh, O., Mandle W.F. and Travers, P. (eds), *Irish Culture and Nationalism 1750-1950* (London: Macmillan in association with Humanities Research Centre, Australian National University, 1983).

Maley, Willie, *The Story of the Celtic* (Glasgow: Villafield Press, 1939).

Mandle, W.F., *The Gaelic Athletic Association and Irish Nationalist Politics, 1884-1924* (London: Christopher Helm Publishers, 1987).

Meehan, Helen, *Inver Parish in History* (Mountcharles: 2005).

Meehan, H. & Duffy, G., *Tracing your Donegal Ancestors* (Dublin: Flyleaf Press, 2008).

MacLaughlin, Jim (ed.), *Donegal – The Making of a Northern County* (Dublin: Four Courts Press, 2007).

Monaghan, Eamonn, *Remembering our founders* (Donegal: CLG Dun na nGall, 1997).

Nolan, W., Ronayne, L. & Dunlevy, M. (eds), *Donegal History and Society: Interdisciplinary Essays on the History of an Irish County* (Dublin: Geography Publications, 1995).

Ó Baoighill, Padraig, *Cardinal Padraig O'Donnell 1856-1927* (Fintown: Chró na mBothán, 2008).

Ó Caithnia, Liam P., *Scéal na hIomana* (Dublin: An Clochomhar Tta, 1980).

Ó Gallchóir, Fr Seán, *The Raidió na Gaeltachta Book of Donegal GAA Facts* (Donegal: Raidió na Gaeltachta, 1996).

Short, Con, *The Ulster GAA Story* (Rossan: Ulster GAA Committee, 1984).

Sugden, J. & Bairner, A., *Sport, Sectarianism and Society in a Divided Ireland* (Leicester: Leicester University Press, 1993).

Sweeney, Frank, *The Murder of Connell Boyle, County Donegal, 1898* (Dublin: Four Courts Press, 2002).

Taylor, Matthew, *The Association Game – A History of British Football* (Harlow: Pearson Education Limited, 2008).

Tranter, Neil, *Sport, Economy and Society in Britain 1750-1914* (Cambridge: Cambridge University Press, 1998).

ARTICLES

Bolger, Pat, 'The congested districts board and the co-ops in Donegal' in Nolan, Ronayne & Dunlevy (eds), *Donegal History and Society: Interdisciplinary Essays on the History of an Irish County* (Dublin: Geography Publications, 1995), pp649-71.

Cronin, Mike, 'Enshrined in blood: the naming of Gaelic Athletic Association clubs and the English influence on Irish sport' in *The Sports Historian*, vol.17, no.2 (Wiltshire: The British society of sports history, 1998), pp90-104.

Cronin, Mike, 'Fighting for Ireland, playing for England? The nationalist history of the Gaelic Athletic Association and the English influence on Irish sport' in *International Journal of the History of Sport*, vol.15, no.3 (London: Frank Cass, 1998), pp35-56.

Cunningham, John B., 'The port of Ballyshannon' in *The Donegal Annual 2000, no.52* (Letterkenny: Browne Printers, 2000), pp7-37.

Garnham, Neal, 'Accounting for the early success of the Gaelic Athletic Association' in *Irish Historical Studies*, vol.xxxiv, no.133 (Dublin: Hodges & Figgis, 2004).

Garnham, Neal, 'The roles of cricket in Victorian and Edwardian Ireland' in *Sporting traditions*, vol.19, no.2 (Australia: Australian Society for Sports History, 2003), pp27-48.

Garnham, Neal, 'Football and identity in pre-Great War Ireland' in *Irish Economic and Social History*, no.28 (Dublin: Economic and Social History Society of Ireland, 2001), pp13-31.

Mac a' Ghoill, Padraig S., 'Cross-country hurling in Ardara' in *CLCG Ard a Ratha* (Ardara, 1980) pp53-7.

Mac a' Ghoill, Padraig S., '100 years of the GAA in Donegal' in *The Donegal Annual 1984, no.36* (Ballyshannon: Donegal Democrat Ltd, 1984), pp89-94.

Mallon, Moira, 'Killybegs Emeralds' in *Dearcadh – the Ardara view 1996-7* (Letterkenny: The Donegal Stationery Co., 1996), pp52-3.

Mandle, W.F., 'The Gaelic Athletic Association and popular culture' in MacDonagh, Mandle & Travers (eds), *Irish Culture and Nationalism 1750-1950* (London: Macmillan in association with Humanities Research Centre, Australian National University, 1983), pp104-55.

Mandle, W.F., 'Sport as politics: the Gaelic Athletic Association 1884-1916' in Cashman & McKernan (eds), *Sport in History* (Brisbane: Queensland University Press, 1979), pp 99-123.

MacLaughlin, Jim, 'The politics of nation-building in post-famine Donegal' in Nolan, Ronayne & Dunlevy (eds), *Donegal History and Society: Inter-disciplinary Essays on the History of an Irish County* (Dublin: Geography Publications, 1995), pp583-621.

Meehan, Helen, 'The MacManus brothers' in *The Donegal Annual 1994, no.46* (Ballyshannon: Donegal Democrat Ltd, 1994), pp5-19.

Metcalfe, Alan, 'Football in the mining communities of East Northumberland, 1882-1914' in *The International Journal of the History of Sport,* vol.5, no.3 (London: Frank Cass, 1988), pp269-91.

Ó Casaide, Seán, 'It was the Gaelic Leaguers who rallied Donegal' in *Irish Press GAA*

Supplement (1934).

O'Hara, Bernard, 'Michael Davitt remembered' in Sean Beattie (ed.), *The Donegal Annual 2007 – Journal of the County Donegal Historical Society* (Letterkenny: Browne Printers, 2007), pp213-218.

Rouse, Paul, 'The politics of culture and sport in Ireland: A history of the GAA ban on foreign games 1884-1971. Part one: 1884-1921', in *The International Journal of the History of Sport*, vol.10, no.3 (London: Frank Cass, 1993), pp333-360.

Rouse, Paul, 'Sport and Ireland in 1881' in Alan Bairner (ed.), *Sport and the Irish: Histories, Identities, Issues* (Dublin: University College Dublin Press, 2005), pp7-21.

Spence, Harry, 'The graveyard at St Conal's church' in *Dearcadh – The Ardara View, Christmas 1992* (Letterkenny: Donegal Stationery & Printing Co., 1992).

Tranter, Neil, 'The Patronage of Organised Sport in Nineteenth-Century Scotland: a Regional Study' in *The Journal of Sports History*, vol.16, no.3 (Washington: The North American Society for Sports History, 1989), pp227-47.

Tunney, John, 'The marquis, the reverend, the grandmaster and the major: Protestant politics in Donegal, 1868-1933' in Nolan, Ronayne & Dunlevy (eds) *Donegal History and Society: Interdisciplinary Essays on the History of an Irish County*, pp675-94.

ONLINE SOURCES

http://www. inishowennews.com
http://www. census.nationalarchives.ie

ABOUT THE AUTHOR

Conor Curran grew up in Ardara, County Donegal. A primary school teacher, he completed his Masters thesis at St Patrick's College Drumcondra and is currently engaged in a PhD at De Montfort University, Leicester. A former county under-21 goalkeeper, he has won two senior Gaelic football championships, leagues and All-Ireland Gaeltachts with Ardara. He lives in Dublin with Jessica.

INDEX